ADA

ESSENTIAL FUNCTION IDENTIFICATION

A Definitive Application of Title I

ADA
ESSENTIAL FUNCTION IDENTIFICATION

A Definitive Application of Title I

Written by
Roger A. Thrush

Presented by
Woody & Holmes, Inc.
An AccessAbility Press Publication

Published by AccessAbility Press,
a division of Woody & Holmes, Inc.

This text is written as a source of information regarding the included subject matters. The primary goal of this text is to educate. For the purposes of example some characters, names, places, dates and incidents used in text are fictitious and any resemblance to actual events or locales or persons, living or dead, is purely coincidental.

AccessAbility Press nor the author are engaged in rendering legal or other professional services. The services of a competent professional should be obtained if legal or other expert assistance is required. Neither the author nor AccessAbility Press shall have liability or responsibility to any person or entity with respect to any loss or damage caused or alleged to be caused, directly or indirectly, by use of the information or applications compiled in this text.

This text is not a reprint of all the information that is otherwise available on the subject matter. It is assumed that the professionals utilizing the applications discussed in this text, augments these applications with related skills, knowledge and experiences. This text should be used only as a guide. Every effort has been made to make this text complete and as accurate as possible. This text contains the most up to date information available on ADA Title-I at the time of this printing.

ISBN: 0-9638200-0-1

Library of Congress Catalog Card Number 93-073190

Printed in the United States of America

ACKNOWLEDGEMENTS

To the numerous individuals who have influenced my work, Thank You. In particular thank you to...

- Paul Johnson and Kathryn Melamed for the developmental work with Job Analyses in industry before it was fashionable.

- Roy Matheson for promoting my "Job Analysis For An Industrial Setting" course across Canada and the United States.

- Debora Holmes and Dana Woody for their commitment to excellence and professionalism in their work with Industry.

- Ruth Lawrence for her patience, diligence and compassion while wordprocessing this book.

- James Alguire of Digital Ink and Ellen Cox for their coordination and extensive creativity with the design and typesetting of this book.

- And, my wife and children, to whom I dedicate this book. Thank You for all of your love, support and encouragement.

PREFACE

July 26, 1992 was the compliance deadline of Title–I for employers with 25 or more employees. Consequently, many employers have been most interested in issues of applicant screening, reasonable accommodations and identification of essential functions.

For the past decade we have consulted with industry, providing comprehensive vocational rehabilitation counseling/case management services to persons with disabilities. Since 1990, we have attended workshops, purchased reference materials, software and talked with "experts" about ADA. On the whole, we had become quite knowledgeable and confident in our understanding of the various aspects of the federal and related state legislation. However, there was still difficulty with identifying, by consensus, the procedural aspects of data gathering , documenting and implementing the ADA legislation. The myriad of written material, verbal discussion and the increasing number of forms published to assist, have been little help in easing confusion and even disillusionment concerning implementation of the ADA legislation. We knew the **who, what, when, where, and even the why** but **how?**— that was the **missing link.**

For all their good intentions, the "experts" providing training and publishing reference material had failed to provide workable applications. It is important that job data be systematically gathered and analyzed in order to develop solutions compatible with the intent of the ADA legislation. Therefore, we surmised, the missing link was the basic methodologies and application systems adaptable to varying employer situations, but still empowering the employer or consultant. No wonder employers were confused and disillusioned. Without specific implementation directives, how were they to meet the federal mandate? The extensive labor costs and/or outside consultant costs prohibited many employers from commencing with the implementation of Title I.

Much to our relief, we discovered that a long time friend and associate had the answer to our **missing link** problem. Author Roger Thrush has performed job data gathering in industry for more than ten years developing and fine tuning his techniques to a science; a science which employs a very common sense and logical approach ensuring a methodology easy to understand and implement. Roger has personally demonstrated and taught these job data gathering techniques to rehabilitation professionals across Canada and the United States.

When he was contracted to teach these techniques to our experienced Vocational Rehabilitation Counselors, he revolutionized their approach toward objectively documenting the physical requirements of specific positions in industry. They came away enlightened and enthused by the demonstrated versatility of the applications and on-site observation techniques he had developed.

As you will see throughout the book, this "how to" guide is based on the Author's experiences. The chapters address the following four steps that are encompassed in his methodology for identifying essential functions.

1. Verify the Purpose for Gathering the Job Data (Chapter 3)

2. Gather Position Specific Data (Chapter 3 and 4)

3. Analyze the Data (Chapter 5)

4. Prepare Documentation (Chapter 6)

He will discuss the importance of the Analyst clearly understanding the purpose of why the job analysis is being conducted, how the job data to be gathered can be separated into five categories, and how each category of data (listed below) can be easily gathered independently of each other.

The categories are:

Job Information

Job Summary

Job Functions

Job Requirements

Job Qualifications

To ensure consistency and a thorough analysis of the job data, Roger Thrush has developed an Essential Functions Criteria Checklist form (Chapter 6). He firmly believes that before analyzing the job data it must be verified as being current, accurate and complete. He cautions against analyzing job class data to identify essential functions and /or to evaluate potential accommodations of a **specific position** within a job class.

The job data gathering and analysis applications in this book are not dependent upon the reader using the Job Analysis Worksheet or the Job Description format. For those with existing documentation forms or software, you may not need to alter the documentation at all. The data gathering and analysis applications are beneficial regardless of the particular form or format used to document the data. If you have not developed any particular job data gathering worksheets or job description formats, those illustrated in the book can be utilized.

AccessAbility Press had one goal in mind in publishing this book and that was providing the user, a step by step, reader friendly guide which accentuates with humor and illustration the dry technical points of this material. It is our hope that after reading this book you will understand the methodology presented and walk away saying "yes, I can do this".

It is our experience that the methodologies and applications illustrated in this book are the most helpful for consultants and employers desiring to properly identify, analyze and document essential functions of positions in industry.

Dana Woody, CRC, CIRS

Debora Holmes, MS, CRC, CIRS

Woody & Holmes, Inc.

AccessAbility Press

ABOUT THE AUTHOR

Roger Thrush received his Master of Science Degree in Rehabilitation Counseling from San Diego State University, San Diego, California in 1980. He is nationally certified as an Insurance Rehabilitation Specialist and Rehabilitation Counselor.

His firm, Job Analysis Specialties, has specialized in conducting job analyses in industry since 1982. Mr. Thrush regularly lectures and teaches certification and continuing education courses for Employment Training Specialists, Vocational Rehabilitation Counselors, Rehabilitation Nurses, Physical Therapists, Occupational Therapists, and Human Resource Personnel across the United States and Canada. In private practice he has consulted and worked with hundreds of public and private sector agencies, corporations and their employees. He has conducted over 3,500 on site job analyses to include task analyses, safety analyses, physical demand analyses, ergonomic analyses, job stress and strain analyses, and job accommodation analyses. Since early 1992, he has provided ADA implementation consultation, training, essential function identification and job analyses to such corporations as General Dynamics, Space Division; Sony Corporation; San Diego Gas and Electric; and San Diego Community College Foundation.

Mr. Thrush was Coordinator of Vocational Rehabilitation benefits for the State Compensation Insurance Fund of San Diego, California, and Coordinator of Vocational Rehabilitation Services for the University of California, Irvine Campus and Medical Center. He is past president of the Association of Industrial Rehabilitation Representatives, past Executive Board member of the American Society of Training and Development—Career Development Division, and for two years he served on the Board of Directors of the California Association of Rehabilitation Professionals. He is frequently called upon to testify in litigated matters as a vocational rehabilitation expert witness.

TABLE OF CONTENTS

For the past two and one half years, I have been teaching across the United States and Canada an introductory course entitled "Job Analysis for an Industrial Setting". In addition to lecturing on job analysis, I have personally performed more than 3,500 job analyses. Physical Therapists, Occupational Therapists, Vocational Rehabilitation Counselors, Program Directors, Human Resource Managers, Rehabilitation Nurses, Functional Capacity Evaluators, Exercise Physiologists, etc. attend the course to learn how to conduct on-site job analyses. These professionals use job analyses for a wide variety of purposes. I believe one of the reasons for the success and wide spread interest in the course has been that it provides the attendee a sound methodology for identifying and quantifying the duties and physical requirements of an individual's work. The methodology is not "how to fill out a form" but how to interview, observe, and document job related data in an efficient and concise manner. The trained Analyst has a high degree of confidence in the objectivity and accuracy of the data collected. The methodology can be applied to any industry for professional, service, trade, agricultural, or governmental occupations.

It is the sole intent and goal of this publication to provide the reader a **methodology** and an understanding of how to conduct job analyses, and prepare job specification **documents** which will identify the essential functions of positions in the work place in compliance with Americans with Disability Act(ADA). The reader will be provided a systematic methodology using proven procedures to timely and efficiently gather, document and verify job related data. This book is a technical manual of how to conduct professional job analyses in industrial settings and identify essential function criteria consistent with ADA-Title I requirements.

Typical situations across the county where a clearer understanding of ADA Title–1 and/or properly conducted job analysis could be impactful are:

Jackie Evans is the Human Resource Manager for a manufacturing company who employs approximately 1,200 unionized employees at two plants. Ms. Evans knows that the existing job descriptions are not current nor have they been updated per ADA-EEOC guidelines. Recently an employee returning from an extensive medical leave of absence requested a job accommodation to facilitate his return to work. Ms. Evans was unsure how to determine if this employee would be able to perform the essential functions of the job with the requested accommodations.

Betty Colby is the owner of a small restaurant employing approximately 20 employees. She has read about ADA Title-I in the trade journals and heard speakers talk about it at Chamber of Commerce meetings. She knows that she has to comply by July 26, 1994. She does not currently have job descriptions or job specification documentation.

Mike Watson, a Vocational Rehabilitation Counselor, has been requested by an employer to provide training in job specific data gathering and document preparation methodologies. The employer wants to be able to prepare job descriptions and specification documents which will comply with the ADA-EEOC guidelines.

Jim Williams, a 42 year old warehouseman, works in the shipping department of a mid-size manufacturer. He strained his lower back on the job. Following a 4 month medical leave of absence, he is requesting to return to work to his prior position, which is still vacant. His doctor has released him to return to work with a permanent work restriction. Mr. Williams is restricted from performing repetitive lifting of heavy objects (more than 50 pounds) and from repetitive bending and stooping activities.

These individuals and others in similar situations across the country could benefit from a clearer understanding of ADA Title-I. Over the past two years there have been seminars, conferences, trade journal articles, training programs and even published manuscripts discussing ADA Title-I issues. In my experience and talking with numerous individuals attending the presentations most walk away with the feeling of having again heard what they have already heard and without a clear methodology or procedures of how to go about implementing a compliance process. EEOC clearly intended to have the professionals in industry develop and implement the specific methodologies required to comply with the essence of ADA Title-I, in consideration of the EEOC Technical Assistance Manual, Interpretive Guidelines and Case Law.

This book reviews several topics, from the ADA legal obligations of employers to the preparation of Job Specification documents. The seven chapters of this book are presented as a guide to the reader. Each chapter has been written to permit it being read independently of the others. It is recommended that the entire book be read. To facilitate the process, a Job Analysis Worksheet and Job Description Form are provided. Examples of the job analysis methodologies are presented on these forms. These forms are not intended to represent the "preferred" or "best" forms for ADA Job Analyses or Job Descriptions. The author developed and uses these forms and have found them easily utilized by novice and experienced Analysts. The methodologies presented can be utilized independent of these interview/data gathering and report writing forms.

Let's begin, in Chapter One, with an overview of the ADA Title–I employment legislation itself. We'll summarize why this legislation was needed and just what it entails.

CHAPTER 1

ADA OVERVIEW

An Overview of the ADA–Title I Employment
Legislation; why it is needed and what it entails.

ADA OVERVIEW

The Americans with Disability Act (ADA) of 1990 was signed into law on July 26, 1990, as Public Law 12101-12213. The purpose of the law is to provide a clear, comprehensive, consistent and enforceable national mandate for the elimination of discrimination against individuals with disabilities.

The Equal Employment Opportunity Commission (EEOC) is the designated enforcement arm for the ADA Title–I provisions. EEOC is also the enforcement agency for Title VII of the Civil Rights Act of 1964, specifically for equal employment opportunity issues. On July 26, 1991, the EEOC published Interpretative Guidelines in the Federal Register Part V, 29CFR Part 1630. In January 1992, EEOC published the Technical Assistance Manual On the Employment Provisions (Title-I) of the ADA. These publications provide the best available interpretative guidance to establish enforceable methodologies for compliance with the understood intent of the Act. Through future case law, more definitive or alternative guidance will be established.

In the process of enacting this legislation, Congress found that discrimination against individuals with disabilities had persisted in such critical areas as:

- Employment
- Public Accommodations
- Transportation
- Recreation
- Health Services
- Access to Public Services
- Housing
- Education
- Communication
- Institutionalization
- Voting

Unlike individuals who have experienced discrimination on the basis of race, color, sex, national origin, religion or age, individuals who have experienced discrimination on the basis of disability have often had no legal recourse to address such discrimination. Some 43 million Americans have one or more physical or mental disabilities. This number is increasing as the population as a whole is growing older. Despite the Rehabilitation Act of 1973 and the enhanced awareness of society regarding the needs of individuals with disabilities, society continues to isolate and segregate these individuals. This form of discrimination continues to be a serious and pervasive social problem.

Individuals with disabilities continue to encounter various forms of discrimination, including:

- Outright intentional exclusion

- Discriminatory architectural barriers

- Societal failure to make modifications to existing policies and practices

- Exclusionary qualification standards and criteria

- Transportation barriers
- Over-protective rules and policies
- Communication barriers
- Segregation and relegation to lesser services, programs, activities, benefits, jobs and other opportunities

Census data and other studies have documented that individuals with disabilities as a group occupy an inferior status in our society and are severely disadvantaged socially, vocationally, economically and educationally.

These individuals with disabilities are subjected to purposeful unequal treatment based on characteristics that are beyond their control. The treatment resulting from stereotypical assumptions is not truly indicative of the individual's ability to participate and contribute productively to society.

The enactment of ADA provides substance to our nation's goals regarding individuals with disabilities; those being to assure equality of opportunity, participation, independent living and economic self sufficiency. The continuing existence of unfair and unnecessary discrimination and prejudice denies individuals with disabilities the opportunity to compete on an equal basis and to pursue those opportunities for which our society provides. The cost to the United States is billions of dollars in unnecessary expenses resulting from dependency and nonproductivity. It is the inherent goal of this legislation to significantly reduce the unnecessary expenses by including this very large population into the mainstream thereby enhancing productivity and reducing dependency.

The ADA is comprised of five sections or titles:

TITLE I - EMPLOYMENT

Prohibits discrimination in the terms and conditions of employment against a qualified individual with a disability.

It was effective on July 26, 1992, for employers with 25 or more employees. On July 26, 1994, it will be effective for employers with 15 or more employees.

TITLE II - PUBLIC SERVICES

Prohibits discrimination by a public entity in providing public services to individuals with a disability. The effective date for services in general was January 26, 1992. The effective date for compliance of new construction activities was January 26, 1993.

TITLE III - PUBLIC ACCOMMODATIONS AND SERVICES OPERATED BY PRIVATE ENTITIES

Prohibits private entities from discrimination against individuals with a disability in providing public accommodations and services. Public accommodations include:

- Places of lodging
- Museums
- Retail stores
- Recreational parks

- Restaurants
- Educational facilities
- Theaters
- General Service establishments

This title also requires that new commercial facilities and public accommodations are designed and constructed so that they are readily accessible to individuals with disabilities, unless it is structurally impractical to do so. Architectural barriers must be removed in existing public accommodations where removal is readily achievable.

Effective dates are:

- January 26, 1992   Public Bus Systems
- January 26, 1992   Public Rail Systems
- July 26, 1995   Public trains, minimum of one accessible car
- January 26, 1992   Private transportation companies
- July 26, 1993   Rail station accessibility

TITLE IV - TELECOMMUNICATIONS

Requires that common carriers of interstate wire or radio communications provide technological accommodations for individuals with hearing and speech impairments. The effective date was July 26, 1993.

TITLE V - MISCELLANEOUS PROVISION

Contains various additional provisions of the ADA. Among the provisions, an individual is prohibited from retaliating against or coercion of an individual who seeks to enforce another's or their own rights under ADA. Title–V also amends sections of the Rehabilitation Act of 1973 to exclude current users of alcohol and drug abuse from its coverage.

EMPLOYMENT PROVISIONS OF ADA

The provisions of Title-I, which employers must incorporate into their employment practices, are discussed in this section. The aspects of these provisions that relate to identification of essential functions and reasonable accommodations of a position are the essences of this book. The author feels that the reader must understand the interpretive guidelines in the legislative provisions of ADA. These guidelines are the foundation for the recommended applications in this book.

The essence of the legislated prohibition of discrimination is best quoted from the law.

"No covered entity shall discriminate against a qualified individual with a disability because of the disability of such individual in regard to job application procedures, the hiring, advancement or discharge of employees, employee compensation, job training and other terms, conditions and privileges of employment."

From this paragraph three terms need additional discussion; *"covered entity"*, *"disability"*, and *"qualified individual with a disability"*.

Covered Entity

The term *"covered entity"* means an employer, employment agency, labor organization, or joint labor-management committee. The term *"employer"* means a person engaged in an industry affecting commerce that has 15 or more employees and any agent of any employer. Employers with 25 or more employees have been required to comply with ADA Title–I since July 26, 1992. Employers with 15 or more employees will be required to comply by July 26, 1994. (Other than the provisions of effective dates in regards to number of employees of an employer, the term "covered entity" is identical in definition as referenced in Section 701 of the Civil Rights Act of 1964).

Disability

The term *"disability"* means with respect to an individual:

(1) A physical or mental impairment which substantially limits one or more major life activities of such individual; or

(2) Having a record of such impairment; or

(3) Being regarded as having an impairment.

1. The first condition in the definition of disability is, *"physical or mental impairment"*. This term means:

(A) Any psychological disorder or condition, cosmetic disfigurement or anatomical loss affecting one or more of the following body systems: neurological, muscular skeletal, special sensory organs, respiratory, cardiovascular, reproductive, digestive, genitourinary, hemic and lymphatic, skin and endocrine; or

(B) Any mental or psychological disorder such as mental retardation, organic brain syndrome, emotional or mental illness and specific learning disabilities. The existence of an impairment is to be determined without regard to use of medicines, assistive or prosthetic devices to accommodate the impairment.

The term *"substantially limits"* means:

(A) Unable to perform a major life activity that the average person and the general population can perform or,

(B) Significantly restricted as to the condition, manner or duration under which an individual can perform a particular
major life activity as compared to the condition, manner or duration under which the average person in the general population can perform the same major life activity.

The factors to consider when determining if an individual is substantially limited in a major life activity include:

(A) The nature and severity of the impairment;

(B) The duration or expected duration of the impairment;

(C) The permanent or long term impact resulting from the impairment.

The term *"major life activities"* means activities that an average person can perform with little or no difficulty such as:

- Caring for one's self
- Walking
- Hearing
- Learning

- Performing manual tasks
- Seeing
- Speaking
- Working

The major life activity of **work** means being significantly restricted in the ability to perform either a class of jobs or a broad range of jobs in various classes. The inability to perform a single particular position may not constitute a *"substantial limitation"* in the major life activity of work. Specific factors to consider in determining whether an individual is substantially limited in the major life activity of work include:

(A) The geographical areas to which the individual has reasonable access,

(B) The position from which the individual has been disqualified because of impairment and the number and types of jobs utilizing similar training, knowledge, skills or abilities within the geographical area from which the individual is also disqualified because of the impairment, and

(C) The position from which the individual has been disqualified because of impairment.

An individual is not substantially limited in working just because the individual is unable to perform in a particular position for one employer or because he or she is unable to perform in a specialized position or profession requiring extraordinary skills, knowledge or experience. If the individual is only unable to perform in either a particular or specialized position or a narrow range of jobs then they would not be substantially limited in the ability to work. However, an individual does not have to be totally unable to work in order to be considered substantially limited in the major life activity of work.

> **For Example:**
>
> An individual who has a back condition that prevents the performance of all heavy laborious jobs would be substantially limited in the major life activity of work because the impairment eliminates s/he from performing a class of jobs.

2. The second condition in the definition of disability is, ***"an individual who has a record of such an impairment."***

   This means a history of or has been misclassified as having a mental or physical impairment that substantially limits one or more major life activities.

   > **For Example:**
   >
   > An individual with a history of mental illness, cancer or heart disease would be considered disabled under ADA.

3. The third condition under the definition of disability is ***"an individual who is regarded as having a disability."*** This includes:

   (A) A physical or mental impairment which does not substantially limit major life activities but is treated by a covered entity as constituting such a limitation.

   > **For Example:**
   >
   > An employee who has controlled high blood pressure that is not substantially limiting but the employer reassigns the individual to less strenuous work because of the unsubstantiated fear that the individual will suffer a heart attack if he or she continues to perform strenuous work. This would be an example of regarding the individual as being disabled.

   (B) As having a physical or mental impairment that substantially limits major life activities only as a result of the attitudes of others toward such impairment.

   > **For Example:**
   >
   > An individual with a facial scar, visible disfigurement or condition that periodically causes an involuntary jerk of the head but does not limit that individual's major life activities. If the employer discriminates against this individual by placing them in non-customer contact positions, the employer would be regarding the individual as being disabled and acting upon the basis of the perceived disability.

(C) Has none of the impairments previously listed but is treated by a covered entity as having a substantially limiting impairment.

For Example:

If the employer discharged an employee in response to a rumor that the employee was infected with Human Immunodeficiency Virus (HIV) even if the rumor was totally unfounded. The employer, by discharging this employee, would be treating the individual as if s/he had a disability. This would be discrimination.

QUALIFIED INDIVIDUAL WITH A DISABILITY

The term *"qualified individual with a disability"* is:

"An individual with a disability who satisfies the requisite skill, experience, education and other job related requirements of the employment position such individual holds or desires and who with or without reasonable accommodation can perform the essential functions of such position."

The employer must determine if the individual with the disability, first of all, has a disability as outlined above and additionally, must determine if the individual is qualified for the position for which they desire or the one they had held.

Once the employer has determined that the individual in question is in fact an individual with a disability (as described above), and there is a vacancy which the individual desires, or an employee desires to return to work to a position (once held) that is otherwise vacant, the employer will need to determine whether the individual with a disability is a *"qualified individual with a disability"*.

It is necessary that the individual with a disability be qualified to perform the essential functions with or without accommodations of the position held or desired. The employer must have gathered the following data to evaluate an incumbent or applicant for the vacant position.

1. What are the qualifications for the position?

2. What are the requirements of performance for the position?

3. What are the essential functions of the position?

4. What reasonable accommodations would be required for the individual to perform the essential functions of the position?

1. Qualifications

The qualifications identified by an employer for the position must be job related and considered to be a business necessity. Qualifications include required skills, experience, abilities, knowledge, education, licenses and credentials.

Per the interpretative guidelines, it is unlawful for the employer to use qualification standards, employment tests or other selection criteria that screen out or tend to screen out an individual with a disability or a class of individuals with disabilities on the basis of disability, unless the standard, test or other selection criteria as used by the covered entity is shown to be job related for the position in question, and is consistent with business necessity.

ADA mandates that an employer ensures that selected and administered tests utilized for employment selection are actually job related. The testing procedure selected for job applicants or employees, who have an impairment, should not deter from evaluating accurately the skills, aptitudes or whatever other factors of the applicant or employee that the test purports to measure.

To show qualifications are job related, the employer should ensure each qualification is required for the performance of particular duty(ies) or task(s). A job analysis of the position in question would best reflect the functions and related qualifications.

2. Requirements

The specific requirements for a position must also be job related and of a business necessity. It would be unlawful for an employer to use standards and criterion selection methods which are not job related nor consistent with business necessity, and that discriminate or that perpetuate discrimination on the basis of disability.

Job analysis methodologies are used to gather data to identify and quantify the requirements of a position. The requirements include:

- Physical demands
- Environmental conditions
- Safety factors, and
- Machine, equipment, tools and work aids utilized

An employer may make pre-employment inquiries into the abilities of an applicant. The employer may ask an applicant to describe or demonstrate how, with or without accommodations, they could perform job related functions. The job analysis identifies and describes the functions and a manner and means for carrying out the functions.

3. Essential Functions

Per the ADA, the term *"essential function"* means:

"The fundamental job duties of the employment position the individual with the disability holds or desires."

The term does not include the marginal duties of the position. The ADA does not require employers to either define jobs or have formal job description documents. ADA does require that the individual's ability to perform the job be measured by an analysis of the essential functions. An employment decision must be based on the persons qualifications to perform the essential functions, not based on their inability to perform marginal function(s).

The identification of essential functions is critical to:

1. The development of accurate and objective job descriptions.

2. Developing appropriate interview questions.

3. Determining whether a candidate or employee can perform such functions, and with what degree of competence.

4. Determining whether or not and to what extent specific job accommodations can be made for a particular individual.

4. Reasonable Accommodations

The employer must determine if the provision of reasonable accommodations would permit the qualified individual with a disability to perform the essential functions of the desired or held position.

The term *"reasonable accommodation"* means;

"Modifications or adjustments to the job application process, to the work environment or the manner or circumstances under which the position held or desired is customarily performed or to enable an employee with the disability to enjoy equal benefits and privileges of employment as are enjoyed by the other employees without disabilities."

Reasonable Accommodations may include:

1. Making existing facilities used by employees accessible,

2. Job restructuring,

3. Part-time or modified work schedules,

4. Reassignment to a vacant position,

5. Acquisition or modifications of equipment or devices,

6. Modifications of examinations, training materials or policies,

7. Provision of qualified readers or interpreters

8. Other similar accommodations for individuals with disabilities.

To determine the appropriate accommodation, it is best to initiate an informal interactive process with the qualified individual with the disability to identify the precise limitations and the necessary reasonable accommodations required to overcome those limitations. Further discussion in Chapter 7.

SUMMARY

The covered entity or employer has the overall responsibility for determining the essential functions, qualifications and requirements for each position and class of jobs.

The individual with a disability seeking employment in a vacant position or returning to work in a previously held position has a responsibility for informing the employer of any impairment and need for accommodations to perform the essential functions of the position. An interactive approach between the employer and the qualified individual with disability will enhance sound human resource management policies, procedures and practices.

The integration of qualified individuals with disabilities into the work force will provide a larger labor pool for the employer as well as enhance the potential for increased profitability by increasing production and quality of services and products.

CHAPTER 2

JOB ANALYSIS AS A HUMAN RESOURCE MANAGEMENT TOOL

The Job Analysis is a significant tool for Human Resource Management, to utilize for compliance with ADA Title–I. The job analysis is the common denominator of information required to integrate the many diverse human resource programs.

JOB ANALYSIS AS A HUMAN RESOURCE MANAGEMENT TOOL

GOVERNMENT REGULATIONS

Employers of the 90's have numerous Federal and State Laws, ordinances and regulations to conform with to carry out their daily business affairs. Employee rights, benefits, safety and selection encompass much of the legislated mandates. A great deal of the controversy over employee rights regarding employment date back to the Declaration of Independence. It states:

"We hold these truths to be self evident, that all men are created equal; that they are endowed by their creator with certain inalienable rights; that among these are life, liberty and the pursuit of happiness."

The Fifth Amendment of the United States Constitution proclaims:

"No person shall be deprived of life, liberty or property without due process of law,... And no state shall deny any person within its jurisdiction the equal protection of the laws."

This due process and equal protection provides the basis for the commonly accepted idea that all persons similarly situated will be treated alike both in the privileges conferred and the liabilities imposed. From these basic foundations of individuals' rights, numerous governmental regulations have been formed to enforce compliance of these rights. Examples of regulations that involve employment issues include:

1. Uniform Guidelines of Employee Selection

2. Equal Pay Act

3. Fair Labor Standards Act, 1938

4. Civil Rights Act, 1964, Title VII

5. Rehabilitation Act, 1973, Title V, Sections 501, 502, 503, 504

6. Occupational Safety and Health Act, 1970 - State Workers' Compensation Laws

7. Americans With Disabilities Act, 1990, Title–I

8. Civil Rights Act, 1991

"WHAT'S" AN EMPLOYER TO DO?

Compliance with ADA Title–I is a responsibility of the employer. The gathering of the data in regard to job duties, qualifications and requirements will fall upon the individual or individuals responsible for the management of the employer's human resources (employees.)

I have performed over 3,500 on-site job analyses. It has been my experience that employers have either never formally gathered job related data, or have generic type "job descriptions". These generic descriptions are not specific to a position but at best represent a class of jobs. The employer prepared "job description" generally will only answer the question of "What" is expected of an incumbent. The job descriptions I have reviewed ranged from very generalized to very detailed procedural documents.

A job description to use as evidence of essential functions should be:

A) developed following completion of an objective job analysis,

B) prepared to represent the actual duties, qualifications and requirements of a position,

C) current,

D) specific and not include ambiguous duties, qualifications or requirements.

A job analysis which focuses on the results or outcome of each function and not solely on the way it is customarily performed will be most helpful for the purposes of ADA essential function identification.

Three common types of job analyses which in and of themselves may not be particularly helpful in determining **essential functions** include:

1. A job analysis that classifies jobs according to the "data, people and things" relationship of position tasks is the customary approach by Vocational Rehabilitation Counselors and those Analysts who subscribe to the U.S. Department of Labor *"Revised Handbook for Analyzing Jobs"* approach.

2. Some job analyses incorporate primarily the knowledge, skills, and abilities necessary to perform a position. This helps to measure the importance of certain skills, knowledge and abilities but does not take into account that individuals with disabilities often can perform essential functions by using other skills and abilities.

3. A job analysis which, according to incumbents or supervisors, rates the importance of general characteristics necessary to perform positions, without linking these characteristics to specific tasks, would not be sufficient to determine whether an individual who has particular limitations could perform an essential function(s) with or without accommodations.

The job analysis process should incorporate the following procedures:

1. Identification of the purpose of the position.

2. Observation of incumbents.

3. Interview of incumbents and supervisors.

4. Reviewed production records/workloads.

5. Determination of the importance of the job functions.

   a. Amount of time spent performing the function.
   b. Consequences if the function is not performed.

6. Identification of the environmental criteria.

7. An understanding of the requested methods of performance.

8. Identification of the skills, knowledge, education and abilities required.

The Human Resource Manager typically has responsibility for planning and implementing several employee management programs as part of the overall corporate planning. These programs may include:

- Recruitment
- Selection
- Placement
- Job Evaluation
- Classification
- Performance Standards
- Training
- Career Planning
- Succession Planning
- Organizational Development
- Work Force Analyses
- Collective Bargaining Negotiations

The job analysis (job related data) is the foundation from which all the Human Resource programs are developed. Regardless of the employer methodology utilized, duties and tasks have to be identified (even if not written down) before any Human Resource programs can be implemented.

It is important to understand, that job related data gathered by job analysis can be used for purposes other than recruitment. The job analysis is the common denominator of information required to integrate the many diverse human resource programs.

Table 2–1 illustrates how Human Resource programs are constructed. The foundation of these programs is the identification of job activities.

HUMAN RESOURCE PROGRAM CONSTRUCTION				
DETERMINE	DESCRIBE	DEVELOP	FORMULATE	ENHANCE
Individual Activities and Position Requirements	Duties, Tasks and Position Performance	Classification and Staff Goals	Qualification Standards and Training Programs	Career Development and Job Value
Who What Where How Much Data People Things Concepts	Purpose Consequences of Error Percentage of Time Performing	Performance Standards Selection Standards Promotion Guidelines Recruitment Policies Compensation Program	Knowledge Education Skills Abilities Experiences Licenses Certifications	Promotions Classifications Assignments

Table 2–1

The gathered job information first **determines** individual activities and requirements in the form of who, what, where, and how much time required. This information is the basis for **describing** each job/position in a job description document. By comparing the job descriptions, a classification system is **developed** which will assist in preparing performance standards, selection and recruitment criteria, qualification standards and career ladders. With greater understanding of the knowledge, skills, abilities and employment qualification criteria required to adequately perform in a position, training programs can be **formulated**. Training can be provided either through on-site programs or formal training schools. Job value will be **enhanced** by career development systems. Employee assignments, classifications and promotions can be predicted and directed to add value to an individual's contribution to the organization.

"HOW" ELSE CAN IT BE DONE?

In my experience, most rehabilitationists, (Vocational Rehabilitation Consultants, Occupational Therapists, Physical Therapists, Rehabilitation Nurses and Rehabilitation Engineers) who perform job analyses are mostly concerned with the "How" aspects of a position. Their goal is to identify, describe, and document the quantifiable and/or observable behaviors required to carry out the position requirements. The "how" aspects of the job include:

- Environmental conditions

- Machines, Equipment, Tools, and Work Aids utilized

- Physical demands

- Mental demands

INTEGRATE THE "HOW" AND "WHAT"

Job analyses intended to assist with ADA Title–I compliance will integrate the worker orientation (how) and the employer orientation (what) in a complete analysis of a position. The purpose of the integrated job analysis is to provide an objective description of the position, not the person working in the position.

A job analysis is a systematic process for gathering, documenting and analyzing information about the duties and responsibilities, skills, knowledge, abilities, physical and mental demands and personal characteristics required to qualify for and carry out the functions of the job. In addition, supporting documentation gathered about a position may include its:

- Purpose

- Placement within the organization

- Relationship to other workers or work groups

- Management of human or material resources

- Consequences of error

- Supervision received

- Work environment

- Working conditions

The employer must select their own method of data gathering. The method selected will depend upon the employer's:

- Purpose or reason for performing the job analyses

- Time and resource constraints

- Intended utility of the data to management

- Desire to integrate the data for multiple applications

- Availability of incumbents, supervisors and experts to perform the data gathering.

In my experience, when consulting with employers that have "job descriptions" on file, they have resisted the reviewing, updating and rewriting of these existing job descriptions. Some of the arguments against rewriting job descriptions are:

1. There is an existing Collective Bargaining Agreement which identifies and outlines the responsibilities of individuals within particular classifications. Employers report this as a legal deterrent for rewriting job descriptions.

2. Large amounts of resources have already been spent on developing extensive classification and compensation systems based upon existing job relationships.

3. The employee pool is too large to perform job analyses due to the unavailability of time, on-site staff, or resources to hire outside consultants.

4. There are numerous facilities and locations of employees which prohibits an expedient or efficient method of researching, updating, creating or rewriting job descriptions.

While these are understandable (or legitimate) arguments it is important to remember a key goal of human resource management is matching people with positions.

A job analysis will assist in human resource planning to promote increased productivity by better matching people and positions. An employer that does not have any documents identifying duties may find it prudent to develop data gathering procedures as a basis for evidence of compliance in light of the potential for discrimination claims under ADA. Additionally by providing improved definitions of job requirements, the job analysis enables management to select, place, develop, train, praise and reward employees in a job related and business necessity manner. In this way, the organization can increase work force productivity thereby increasing the quality of its products and services.

What Are Some Job Data Management Alternatives?

Below are five alternatives for the employer to consider as opposed to the "all at one time" expenditures of time, staff and finances required to gather, document, verify, update and analyze positions.

1.) Rather than rewriting all of the existing job descriptions, an addendum could be prepared to attach to each existing job description. The addendum would include the required job related data not included in the existing job description. The addendum could be prepared primarily for recruitment of employees, and also be used as a source of evidence in regard to issues under the ADA. The addendum could be prepared on a position by position basis prior to recruitment for the specific position. Or, addendums could be prepared for those positions or job classes in which there is high exposure in regard to loss of work time due to injury or illnesses. In this way the gathering of the information could be done on an as needed basis, thereby reducing the time required to prepare large numbers of documents and the extensive time involvement of incumbents and supervisors.

2.) Human Resource Management policies, procedures and practices could also be revised. Polices and practices could include a regular and formal review of existing job descriptions for accuracy. It has been my experience that job description updating is not a high priority in most

Human Resource departments. If the job descriptions were regularly reviewed in the course of reviewing compensation systems, union contract negotiations or when developing annual goals and objectives of the organization, it would ensure accuracy of the job information being used for planning by Human Resource Management.

3.) When requested to begin a recruitment, the Human Resource department could either prepare the addendum as discussed above and/or have the existing job description and addendum reviewed by the requesting department for accuracy. This will again ensure that the information provided prior to the recruitment or placement is available and accurate.

4.) Upon notification, by the Benefits Department, that a medical leave of absence has been requested, consider at this time to verify, update and or prepare the addendum for that person's position. In this manner, being prepared for the possibility that the individual may request accommodations to return to work.

5.) The Human Resource Department could prepare a folder which would include the class description. Also recruitment advertising data could be compiled with the job class and position information, thereby over time developing an entire collection of the position descriptions within the job class as well as a history of recruitment and placement policies and practices within a job class.

EXAMPLES:

Remember restaurant owner, Betty Colby, who was one of the examples in the introduction? She could schedule perform job analyses over the year prior to the date of required compliance, thereby extending the expenditure of resources over a longer period of time. She would likely discover numerous benefits from performing job analyses, such as prepared job descriptions, identification of job qualifications, development of classification systems, determining the need for training, and an enhanced understanding for management of her human and financial resources.

Also, Jackie Evans, the Human Resource Manager you met earlier, would be prudent in implementing a practice to ensure being notified by the Benefits Department of individuals out on extended leave, and of positions with high rates of absenteeism or frequent medical leaves. She could commence gathering job related data to update and verify the accuracy of existing job descriptions. She may consider performing job analyses to gather data not included in existing job descriptions, such as physical demands, mental demands and environmental criteria.

Summary

Again, the legislated mandate to ensure equal employment opportunities and privileges for job applicants and employees fall upon the employer. Employers can no longer minimize the organizational benefits and business necessity to have gathered and documented job related data. The current understanding of the law does not "require" an employer to perform job analyses nor prepare job descriptions. However, the requirement for the employer to be able to identify and verify essential functions of a position nearly mandates that they have performed organizational wide job related data gathering and documentation.

In the following three chapters methodologies for data gathering and documentation are discussed. In Chapter 3, interviewing techniques are reviewed. In Chapter 4, new innovative techniques for observing, determining and quantifying the job requirements are outlined. And, in Chapter 5, the preferred method of writing a duty sentence to complete the job description report is demonstrated. A job analysis worksheet and job description report format are introduced. They are used by example throughout these chapters. The goal of this book is to provide you a working model to use when conducting job analyses and preparing job description documents.

CHAPTER 3

DATA GATHERING PROCEDURES— INTERVIEWING TECHNIQUES

Techniques for conducting interviews to gather and document data for defining essential functions and qualifications required in specific positions.

DATA GATHERING PROCEDURES—INTERVIEWING TECHNIQUES

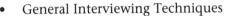
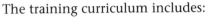

Mike Watson, Vocational Rehabilitation Counselor, and one of the examples used in the introduction, has contracted to train the human resource personnel of an employer in data gathering methodologies. They want to learn how to gather, analyze, and verify the duties, qualifications, and requirements of the work of their employees. After gathering the data, they plan to prepare job function descriptions and specification documents.

The training curriculum includes:

- General Interviewing Techniques

- How to use the Essential Functions—Demands Job Analysis Worksheet

- Scheduling Supervisors and Incumbents for Interview

- Gathering Job Related Information

- Clarifying the Purpose of a Position

- Identifying the Duties and Tasks

- Verifying the Position Related Qualifications

Identifying, quantifying and verifying the requirements (physical demands and environmental conditions) of a position will be discussed in Chapter 4—Observation Techniques.

GENERAL INTERVIEWING TECHNIQUES

The Interview—Observation methodology is most widely accepted and highly recommended for conducting job analyses in the industrial setting. Positions are analyzed by observing workers performing the work and interviewing workers, supervisors, and others who have information pertinent to the position. It is the most desirable method for conducting job analyses because it:

(a) Involves first hand observation by the Analyst;

(b) Enables the Analyst to immediately evaluate the interview data, and;

(c) Permits demonstration and explanation of the various functions of the position.

The Analyst commences the interview in two ways:

(a) Observes a worker performing a complete work cycle before asking any questions. During the observation, the Analyst takes notes of all the activities, including those not fully understood. When satisfied, the worker and supervisor are interviewed.

(b) Observes and interviews simultaneously. Watches and talks with the worker about what is being performed and asks questions about the activities. The Analyst takes notes to record all the data pertinent to the work.

The goal of the interview is to gather, clarify, and verify the position information with knowledgeable individuals. It is assumed that the most knowledgeable individuals are the incumbents who actually perform the position duties and the direct supervisor who evaluates and monitors the incumbent.

The interview process is a conversational interaction between individuals. The objectivity of information received is dependent upon the Analyst's limited contribution of facts to the interview. The Analyst's contribution is based on his/her ability to accurately understand and record the work activities being discussed and observed.

In order for the Analyst to obtain facts quickly, accurately, and comprehensively, it is helpful to have completed and documented all background information prior to the interview. The Analyst is responsible for directing the participants efficiently and painlessly through the interview process, while at the same time remaining objective and friendly.

Using a pre-prepared interview worksheet, (an example is illustrated in this book) will ensure your notes are organized logically, according to the categories of information required for completion of the job analysis report. It is recommended a clipboard be used as a hard surface , so that you can combine note taking with the conversational aspect of the interview in the work area.

I want to introduce a sample interview worksheet prior to discussing a 5 step model for preparing for and conducting job data gathering interviews.

THE ESSENTIAL FUNCTIONS—DEMANDS JOB ANALYSIS WORKSHEET

It has been my experience that most Analysts have difficulty conducting a job site analysis for two reasons:

1) they do not know specifically why a job analysis report is being prepared,

2) they use one "generic" type job analysis interview worksheet for all types of job site analyses.

A different interview worksheet is necessary for conducting job site analyses whenever there is a different purpose. The worksheet should be specifically designed to support (by type of data gathered) the reason for conducting the job analysis.

It is prudent for interviewers to have prepared themselves by developing a list of questions prior to beginning an interview. The interview worksheet is the Analyst's guide for gathering and documenting job related data. The questions on the interview worksheet need to be relevant to the purpose for conducting the job analysis. A thorough, logical and specific–to–the–purpose interview worksheet is the most important component for implementing the Interview—Observation methodology.

Table 3–1 below illustrates different types of job analyses and their purpose. With each type of job analysis the interview worksheet may be slightly or significantly different.

TYPE OF JOB ANALYSIS	PURPOSE
Industrial Injury	Historical perspective of a specific individual's position to determine the usual and customary requirements.
Occupational Health and Safety	Current identification of worker exposures to determine potential for injury or illness.
Ergonomic	Evaluation of workers performance in the workstation and environment.
Human Resource	1. Identify responsibilities to classify positions into job classes. 2. Identify necessary qualifications to develop employment criteria. 3. Identify essential functions for future consideration of reasonable accommodations for qualified individuals.

Table 3-1

Per the EEOC Technical Manual and Interpretive Guidelines, there are no particular formats required to be used for purposes of an ADA job analysis. The job analysis process is necessary to collect and analyze specific position information. The focus of the job analysis should be on the results or outcome of a particular function and not solely the way it is customarily performed.

EEOC suggests that the position related data collected should minimally include the following categories of information:

- Purpose of the job

- Production records

- Interview—Observation data from workers and supervisor(s)

- Importance of individual job functions

- Methods of performance of the essential functions

- Amount of time spent performing the essential functions

- Consequences if essential functions were not performed

- Environmental conditions

- Qualifications required

- Number of workers in work unit

The job analysis interview worksheet should minimally include questions regarding the above categories of information. There are numerous examples of interview worksheets in the current literature. This author has developed and has provided in this book, an interview worksheet for the purpose of gathering and organizing job related data to identify the essential functions, qualifications and requirements of individual positions. The job analysis interview worksheet is provided for use by the reader. It should be modified if the Analyst's specific purpose does not require as extensive an interview or additional information (not listed) is required.

The job analysis interview worksheet displayed throughout this book integrates data collection methodologies from the U.S. Department of Labor, "Revised Handbook for Analyzing Jobs", State of California Worker's Compensation Labor Codes, the author's "Job Analysis for an Industrial Setting" training manual and the author's 10 years of experience as a Job Analyst, Human Resource Consultant and Trainer/Lecturer.

The *"Essential Functions—Demands Job Analysis Worksheet"* is an interview-documentation form categorically divided into five sections. These sections are entitled:

- Job Information

- Job Summary

- Job Functions

- Job Requirements

- Job Qualifications

The job analysis worksheet is designed to be completed as a whole or divided into three worksheets.

1. Job Functions

2. Job Requirements

3. Job Qualifications

The Analyst can choose to gather all the job data or only that portion necessary to augment existing data or records. For example, if a job description has already been prepared, then perhaps only the job requirements need to be clarified for the specific position. Regardless of which section is completed, the **"Job Information** and **Job Summary"** sections on page one should be completed and attached to the sections of the worksheet utilized.

Following is an introduction and explanation of the "Essential Functions - Demands Job Analysis Worksheet". Clarifications not specifically defined on the worksheet or in the following text are necessary to ensure an accurate understanding of the "keys" and purpose of some portions of the worksheet.

On page one, the section labeled **"Production or Workload"** is intended to allow any pre-established quantities of work expectations to be documented. If a worker is expected to inspect, produce, assemble, machine, etc., a specified quantity per minute, day, week, month, or year, it should be stated as specifically as possible.

For example:

"The lapping machine operator is expected to accurately polish 2040 rings per 8 hour shift operating two Speed Fam lapping machines."

Under **"Job Requirements—Physical Factors"** a key is used to define the frequencies of performing the stated requirements. The frequencies are:

NP	Not Present
O	1/3 of the day
F	1/3 to 2/3's of the day
C	Over 2/3's of the day

The codes are defined as:

O	Occasional
F	Frequent
C	Continuous

To determine the frequency of an activity consider, first, the length of the workday. Most workdays are 8, 8-1/2 or 9 hours long. The frequencies selected will not include the AM/PM breaks of normally 10 to 15 minutes each, nor the lunch breaks of normally 30 minutes to 1 hour each. It is assumed that a worker performs productive activity for 7 or 8 hours per day excluding the break times. To determine frequencies, only calculate the productive work time, do not include the break and lunch times. If a workday is 8 hours then the frequency codes would be represented as follows:

O		0 to 3 hours
F		3 to 5 hours
C		5 to 8 hours

To determine the frequency category for an activity it is necessary to calculate the time spent per activity to quantify that activity over the course of the day.

For example:

A worker may perform the activity of climbing up/down a ladder several times over the course of the 8 hour workday. Each climb of approximately 20' requires one to two minutes up, then one to two minutes down. The time spent standing on the ladder to work is not considered climbing but would be part of the frequency category for standing. If it was determined that the worker went up/down the ladder an average of twice per hour the calculation to determine the frequency would be as follows:

2 mins. x 2 times per hour = 4 minutes per hour
4 mins. per hour x 8 hours per day = 32 mins. per day
32 mins. per day (less than 3 hours) = Occasional activity

This approach is acceptable as an accurate calculation, without actually performing a time and motion study over several full workdays of several workers performing in the position(s) being analyzed.

Under the **Physical Factors—Factor 1: Strength, Mobility** section, Table 3–2 will assist in clarifying the relationship between percent (%) of time, hours per day and frequencies (NP, O, F, C).

Remember this calculation of frequency is based on the performance of the activity over the course of the whole workday, not only the length of performance per occurrence. The actual calculation would be the same as discussed above.

Table 3–2

FREQUENCY	HOURS PER DAY	% OF TIME
N/P	0	0
O	Up to 3 hours	Up to 33%
F	3 to 5 hours	33% to 66%
C	5 to 8 hours	66% to 100%

Under **Factor 6—Talking, B. Verbal Contact with Others** means communication with others without face-to-face contact. For example use of telephone, two way radio, computer modem, etc. C. **Public** refers to talking to the general public in the course of performing daily work activity, as would a receptionist, salesperson, information clerk, etc.

Under **Job Requirements, Physical Factors 1, 2, 3, 4, 5, 6, and 7**, the worker actions listed and the **Environmental Factors** are defined in detail in Appendix D.

In the **Safety Factors** section, there is reference to **"Material Safety Data Sheets" (MSDS).** Every employer is mandated by federal Occupational Health and Safety (OSHA) laws to have MSDS's on file for substances to which employees are exposed. The manufacturer of the substance has to provide an MSDS, upon request, to employers. The MSDS identifies the chemical composition of the substance, acceptable exposure parameters, safety equipment recommended, first aid for over–exposure, and related type of data. These are very helpful in employee training and describing work related chemical exposures.

In the **Machines, Equipment, Tools and Work Aids (METW/A)** section, there is a "key". When performing the job analysis, the devices or implements used by the worker are to be listed. For each item listed, it should be noted if prior experience (skill) is required or whether the worker could be taught how to use the item after being hired (on-the-job training). With either selection, the worker would have to be able to use the item listed to perform the intended work activity. Numerous "reasonable accommodations" are provided with the selection or modification of the METW/A used to perform the intended work activity.

In the **Job Qualifications, Mental Factors** portion of the worksheet, the terms, **"Present", "Not Present"** are used to identify the qualifications necessary for performance in the position. The term **"Present"** means that the qualification is required to adequately carry out the essential functions. For example, under **Factor 1—General Education Development**, there are four categories. Under each category except Reasoning, select only one choice—Complex Skills or Simple Skills. Select the one choice that best represents the necessary qualifications to adequately carry out the essential functions. Under the Reasoning Category, more than one and maybe all the choices may be required in the position. At least one must be selected.

The worker actions listed under the **Factors 5, 6, 7, and 8**, are each defined in detail in Appendix D.

For best interviewing results it is important that the Analyst have a working knowledge of their worksheet and a working interpretation of each category of information to ensure consistency in analyzing jobs.

CONDUCTING THE ON–SITE INTERVIEW

To conduct the interview, the Analyst follows a **five step** sequence of data gathering, modifying as necessary for the situation at hand. The **five steps** are:

1. Arranging and commencement of the interview.

2. Gather, verify, and clarify the preliminary information learned or needed about the organization, position or employee(s).

3. Verify and clarify the purpose of the position to be analyzed (the reason it exists in the organization).

4. Identify and verify the duties and tasks of the position to be analyzed.

5. Identify and verify the qualifications relevant to performance in the position.

STEP ONE—ARRANGING AND COMMENCEMENT OF THE INTERVIEW

A properly scheduled site visit will enhance the success of the interview and analysis of the position(s) being analyzed.

The selection of incumbents and supervisors to participate in the interview will vary with the size of the labor pool, size of the job class, and the geographic area where the positions are located. Whenever possible, the incumbents or supervisors should be randomly chosen. They need to be sufficiently trained and experienced in the work they represent. Workers new in the position may not be familiar with all the functions of the position. Senior workers may not have acclimated to new methods and therefore be resistive to detailing their manner and means of performing the duties. They may insist on the method they are familiar with.

Once identified, the specific individual(s) with whom the job analysis will be performed, should be contacted to verify a date and time. Additionally, they should be provided an explanation regarding the purpose of the job analysis, procedures for conducting the job analysis and time requirements. The participants should also be informed that they will receive a copy of the completed analysis for their review.

When scheduling the job analysis, plan on visiting the work site on the shift(s) in which the work is performed. It is also necessary to be at the work site when the essential functions of the position are being performed and can be observed.

The Analyst should request that the supervisor be prepared to provide a description of the position, functions, requirements and, if necessary, an orientation or tour of the department. Written documentation such as an organizational chart, job description, production records and training documents related to the position should be obtained at this time. The Analyst should become familiar with the overall operation so as to best understand how the specific position fits into the organizational/department flow of work. The Analyst should also obtain information such as titles of other positions within the department, number of workers in the department, and the function or outcome goals of the specific position being analyzed to the department and organization as a whole.

Upon arrival to the scheduled on-site visit, the Analyst must take the responsibility for the **commencement** of the interview. A good technique for starting the interview is to;

- Introduce the participants

- Clarify the purpose for conducting the job analysis

- Verify the time frame for the scheduled on-site visit

- Explain the job analysis methodology– emphasizing the participants' role

- Explain what the Analyst is not interested in analyzing the outcome goal

- Ask the participants if they have any questions or scheduling conflicts

Verify authorization for photographing the work during the observation period, if applicable. Remind the participants that they will be provided the written report to read and verify as an accurate representation of the position analyzed. This initial **introduction** should not take more than two to five minutes to complete.

Explain that the **purpose** of the job analysis is to gather job related data to better match assignments and workers. The data collected will be analyzed to determine the essential functions, qualifications and requirements necessary to adequately perform the assigned work. It is important to emphasize that the **outcome goal** of the ADA job analysis is not a compensation study, a safety analysis for a union negotiation, a performance evaluation, a time and motion study, an injury investigation, nor will it reflect negatively upon the participants.

Make the purpose of the interview clear to the participants. Explain briefly why the interview was scheduled, what is expected to be accomplished, how long the interview will take, and why and how the workers' cooperation will help in the preparation of the job analysis report. Dismiss any misunderstanding of the purpose of the job analysis. Encourage the workers to contribute by showing a sincere interest in what they say by reminding them of why their comments are important. It is most important to establish rapport and open communication before commencing the formal interview.

Prior to beginning the formal interview, show the participants the interview worksheet to familiarize them with the general **scope of the interview**. Explain that they or coworkers will be observed carrying out the functions discussed. The interview **time frame** should be 45 minutes to two hours depending on the complexity of the position, attentiveness of the participants, prior knowledge of the work by the Analyst, the ability of the participants to verbally communicate and the interviewing skills of the Analyst. With familiarity of the work and the interview worksheet plus interviewing experience, the actual interview time will decrease.

Once the selected participants are comfortable with and agreeable to **the interview**, the Analyst should address the worker(s) to discuss his/her duties. To ensure accurate and detailed information assist the worker(s) to think and talk according to the logical sequence of the duties performed. Ask the worker(s) to explain the cycle or schedule of duties performed. If duties are not performed in a regular order, ask the worker(s) to describe the duties in a functional manner by taking the most important activity first, the second most important next, and so forth. Request the worker(s) to describe the infrequent duties of the position, or ones that are not a part of the regular activities, such as the occasional set up of a machine, occasional repairs, or infrequent preparation of reports. Infrequently performed duties, however, should not include unknown, periodic or emergency activities.

Allow the worker(s) sufficient time to formulate an answer for each question. The worker(s) should be asked only one question at a time. Do not ask the worker(s) yes or no or leading questions. The interviewer should have the worker(s) and supervisor doing most of the talking, with the Analyst taking notes and clarifying the information discussed.

It is most important to secure the specific and complete information required to completely analyze the position. Control the interview with respect to the economic use of time and adherence to subject matter. When the interviewees stray from the subject, a good technique for bringing them back to the point is to summarize the data collected up to that point. The interview should be conducted patiently and with consideration for any nervousness or lack of ease on the part of the workers or supervisor. Throughout the interview, encourage the supervisor and worker(s) to participate. Obtain clarification and verification of the information provided by the worker(s). At the end of the interview, summarize the information obtained, repeating the major duties performed and the specific information obtained for each of the duties.

MISCELLANEOUS DO'S AND DON'TS FOR INTERVIEWS

1. Do not take issue with the worker(s) or supervisor's statements.

2. Do not show any partiality to grievances or conflicts concerning the employer-employee relationship.

3. Do not show any opinions regarding the wage classification for the position.

4. Show politeness and courtesy throughout the interview.

5. Do not "talk down" to the worker(s).

6. Do not permit yourself to be influenced by your personal likes and dislikes.

7. Be impersonal. Do not be critical or attempt to suggest any changes or improvements in the organization or methods of work during the interview.

8. Only talk to the worker(s), whom are not scheduled to be interviewed, with the permission of the supervisor.

9. Verify job data, especially technical or trade terminology, with the individuals interviewed.

10. Review and verify the completed job analysis report with the individuals interviewed.

11. If the completed report will be verified by officials other than those interviewed, arrange to summarize the findings of the job analysis interview with those officials prior to preparing the narrative report.

STEP TWO—GATHERING PRELIMINARY INFORMATION

All job related information gathered or obtained prior to the scheduled interview should be reviewed with the participants. Information not previously obtained, but needed is gathered from the participants at the beginning of the interview. All the gathered data is written onto the interview worksheet.

By example: The information written onto page one of the *Job Analysis Worksheet* under, **"Job Information."** Specific job information obtained may include the following:

*   Job title

*   Job code

*   Individuals interviewed, by name

- Union Affiliation

- Number of co-workers in the work unit or department

- Salary data

- Department—Work Unit

- Work shift assignment

- Personnel data (if needed, date of hire, promotional dates, medical leave dates, training, certifications, etc.)

- Job description (reviewed, updated or not available.)

Gathering and/or verification of this preliminary information should not require more than ten minutes to complete.

Example: (A warehouse worker position will be used to illustrate this methodology.)

ESSENTIAL FUNCTIONS–DEMANDS JOB ANALYSIS WORKSHEET

Date _3-16-93_   Job Analyst _R. THRUSH_

JOB INFORMATION

Title _WAREHOUSE WORKER_   Employer _ABC DISTRIBUTION CENTER_

Job Code _738-01_   Labor Grade _4_   Salary/Rate _6.95 PER HR._

Department _RECEIVING_   Shift Assignment: A _____   B _X_ C _____

Work Unit _DOCK_   Number Of Employees _4_

Union Affiliation _NONE_

Supervisor(s) _____   Phone No(s). _____

JACK BARLEY   _000-0000_

Incumbent(s) _____   Badge/SSN _____

HENRY CAPPS   _00349_

Job Description: Reviewed ___X___   To Update _____   Not-Available _____

STEP THREE—CLARIFYING THE PURPOSE OF THE POSITION

Identification, clarification and verification of the purpose of the position and why it exists in the organization is critical to establish very early in the interview process. Without clearly understanding the purpose for the position to exist, there is no basis to evaluate, prioritize, quantify importance, or determine criticalness of performance of the position duties and tasks.

The purpose of a position is generally not very difficult to identify. For many positions the job title itself labels the overall purpose. Some examples are:

- Water Tank Cleaner
- Panel Installer
- Window Repairer
- Sales Route Driver
- Boatbuilder
- Lawn Sprinkler Installer

For other positions the materials, machinery or equipment utilized identifies the purpose. Some examples are:

- Cement Truck Driver
- Drill Press Operator
- Arc Welder
- Diesel Engine Repairer
- Glazier
- Bus Driver
- Painter
- Bricklayer
- Plasterer
- Insecticide Mixer

For some positions, the intended outcome or results of the assigned duties identifies the purpose of the specific position. The Analyst can ask questions such as:

- To what or whom is the object of the worker's actions?
- What is the specific action performed? or,
- What would happen if the worker action did not take place?

The statement of purpose can generally be started with the word "to" plus the answer to one of these questions. Some examples are in Table 3–3.

Position	Purpose
Custodian	To ensure assigned areas are clean, safe and secure.
Assembler	To pretest fabricated electrical harnesses.
Environmental Control Technician	To ensure compliance with the heating, ventilation and air conditioning requirements in the specified area.
Fabricator	To fabricate and repair structures using sheetmetal, steel, and fiber-glass.
Calibration Technician	To calibrate mechanical measuring devices.
Final Mechanical Inspector	To ensure mechanical systems conform to engineering data.
Industrial Electrician	To ensure all 28 to 480 volt equipment and electronic circuitry controls are maintained and operable.

Table 3–3

Verifying or determining the purpose of the position to be analyzed should not require more than five to ten minutes.

Example:

JOB SUMMARY

Reason the position exists (purpose):

The purpose of this position is to _RECEIVE, MARK, STORE AND SORT MERCHANDISE PER ESTABLISHED PROCEDURES._

Production or Workload

MAINTAIN A PACE APPROPRIATE FOR THE DAILY WORKLOAD.

STEP FOUR—IDENTIFYING THE FUNCTIONS (DUTIES AND TASKS)

The definition of work is, **"Effort directed toward the production or accomplishment of something; labor"**. Work is the culmination of a broad range of operations performed by an individual to produce goods and/or services. The individual is the basic indivisible physical unit of an organization which performs quantifiable functional tasks of the organization.

Types of work are labeled by their functional duties and tasks. Categorically, work functions are divided into five segments. The segments are convenient for sorting and labeling the vast types of work. The segments are:

- Occupational Group

- Job Class

- Position

- Duty

- Task

It is necessary when analyzing work functions to have a clear understanding of the differences between these terms. I have found that Analysts have a very difficult time, in practice, correctly labeling or distinguishing between an Occupational Group, Job Class, position, duty or task. It is not surprising, because employers have not necessarily correctly labeled their job classes or positions.

For example:

An electronics manufacturer may have labeled all of their production workers as "Assemblers". By investigation, it is determined that this label is correct as an Occupational Group, but as a Job Class the workers are "Electronic Assemblers", and position-to-position they are Chassis Assemblers, Cable Splicers, Face Plate Assemblers, Inspectors, Repairers, Testers, etc. Each of these positions may have several workers performing the same duties and tasks but assigned to different product lines. This labeling problem is compounded for an Analyst because another electronics manufacturer may have "job descriptions" for each position category but not acknowledge a specific Occupational Group or Job Class label.

In public sector agencies, I find the very broad and general approach to labeling work more prevalent.

For example:

There may be one job description titled "Construction Trades". This is intended to represent all the Painters, Carpenters, Electricians, Plumbers, Locksmiths, Masons, etc., regardless of their assignments. However, with further investigation it is discovered that an individuals' actual work functions, even within one trade category, are vastly different. In the painting trade, for example, there may be Interior Painters, Exterior Painters, Spray Painters, Job Schedulers, Crew Leaders, Supervisors, etc. In this situation, the **Occupational Group** is *construction trades*, the **Job Class** is *painter* and the **position titles** are specific to the regularly assigned *duties* and *tasks*, (as listed above).

Another inconsistency found in work labels are the various levels of management/supervision and the levels between positions based on acquired competencies. For example, one employer may have a job description for the generic positions of Manager, Supervisor, Foreman, Leadperson, etc., regardless of their assignment. Another employer may have specific job descriptions for each supervisory position assignment. The same mind set is found with employers who label competency levels such as; Apprentice, Journeyman, Trainee, Helper, Senior, I, II, III, etc.

As an Analyst, it is necessary to correctly label a position before attempting to analyze it. It may be necessary to analyze a group of positions to determine the different Job Classes and Occupational Groups. It is mandatory that the Analyst clearly understand where the duties and tasks of each position begin and end. It is not necessary for the employer to accept the Analyst's labels, however each function, qualification and requirement of a position, job class, and occupational group, should be analyzed, documented and defined according to each employer situation encountered by the Analyst.

Below is a brief definition for each segment.

Occupational Group

An occupational group may consist of several job classes which are similar in terms of the experience, training, and types of skills, knowledge and abilities required of the workers. An occupational group involves an entire category of work, without regard to level or grade.

Job Class

A job class is a group of identical positions which are very similar in their significant duties. A job class may be defined by a group of positions with the same level or grade. While a distinction is made between job class and position, the terms are often used interchangeably.

Position

A position consists of the duties requiring the activities of only one worker. Positions may vary in scope and purpose but each has distinguishing characteristics. There are as many positions as there are workers.

The characteristics of a position are:

- It has a definite scope and purpose

- It requires the full time activities of one individual

- It involves work which usually utilizes related skills knowledge and abilities

- It is usually established and formally recognized on an organizational table/chart

- It exists whether occupied or vacant

Each position is defined in scope and purpose primarily by the skills, knowledge and abilities required of a worker to perform its' duties and tasks. In other words, it is the distinctive duties and tasks of a position that distinguishes it from other positions, job classes and occupational groups.

Duty

A duty encompasses a large segment of the work activities performed by an individual. Each duty may encompass any number of tasks.

A duty is a distinct and major activity involved in the work performed or required of each position. The distinguishing characteristics of a duty are:

- It is usually recognized as a principal responsibility of the position

- It occupies a reasonable portion of the work time

- It occurs with reasonable frequency in the work cycle

- It involves tasks which utilize related skills, knowledge and abilities

- It is performed for some purpose, by some method, according to some standard with respect to speed, accuracy, quality or quantity

Task

A task is a distinct and identifiable work activity that constitutes one of the logical and necessary steps in the performance of each duty of a position.

The distinguishing characteristics of a task are:

- It occupies a reasonable portion of the work time spent in performing a duty

- It involves activities with closely related skills, knowledge and abilities

- It is performed according to some standard

The U.S. Department of Labor's publication "Dictionary of Occupational Titles (DOT) 1991 Edition" is a very good example of categorical labeling. You may want to review this document strictly for the purpose of further studying the work labeling techniques. (Do not expect or try to identify in the DOT, work categories for specific employers, or label work found at specific employers directly to the DOT. The DOT is only intended to be a reference of nationally recognized Occupational Groups and duty functions. It is not a definitive statement of what these groups or functions should be. I strongly encourage the analyst not to depend upon the DOT data base as an alternative source for analyzing specific employer positions.)

In the DOT, all types of work are organized into Occupational Groups. Within each group are specific Job Classes or categories. Within the description of each Job Class, alternate titles (positions) are identified. For example, the Occupational Group–076–is "Therapists". The Job Classes which make up this Occupational Group are similar in that they medically treat and rehabilitate people with physical and/or mental disorders to restore functions and maintain optimum performance. One of the Job Classes is "Physical Therapist" (.014). Position titles include Physiotherapist, Pediatric Physical Therapist, Pulmonary Physical Therapist, Research Physical Therapist, Supervisor, Director or Manager. There are also Physical Therapist Aides and Assistants. Individual Physical Therapists may be labeled according to a particular type of therapy provided, disorders treated, or their role within an organization.

When conducting a job analysis in the industrial setting, a specific position which is distinguishable from other positions of the same job classification or occupational group is most frequently analyzed. It must be recognized that each incumbent interviewed represents a separate position.

The Analyst must be able to determine what the specific duties are in the sense of where they begin and where they end. The Analyst may need to analyze a group of positions (Job Class) or an entire occupational group to determine the number of positions existing before examining the exact nature of one position. A position should be analyzed as it exists and not as the Analyst would think it should exist or as it may exist in other establishments.

The Analyst may want to consider the following four situations when seeking to identify and verify the critical duties/tasks of a position.

1. If the worker performs a specific cycle or sequence of functions, the Analyst should identify the cycle or sequence from beginning to end.

2. Functions could be organized according to the key functions and prioritized according to significance or criticalness to the position.

3.   If the worker frequently changes from one set of functions to another, the functions could be organized according to a time schedule.

4.   Functions may vary and not follow a sequence or schedule. In this case, the critical functions should be listed without regard to priority.

DATA GATHERING ALTERNATIVES

In some instances, it is impossible to use the Interview—Observation method as discussed. The worker may not be observed performing the tasks because of security reasons, reluctance on the part of management to allow the Analyst to observe the manufacturing process, or the complex and protracted nature of the work. In other instances, it may be impossible to interview the worker while observing the activities because of the surrounding noise or the manager's request not to disturb other workers. A large number of positions, such as those in professional and technical areas, do not lend themselves to the interview and observation method since they do not involve a set sequence of tasks, and therefore cannot be observed as an entire unit.

In these cases the Analyst should consider:

(1)   using establishment job descriptions or specifications supplemented by discussions with administrative and technical personnel;

(2)   obtaining job descriptions, specifications, hiring requirements, and related data for the positions from associations, societies, and other similar organizations; or

(3)   interviewing workers and supervisors at the worksite, without the benefit of observing the duties and tasks.

The Analyst's purpose, regardless of the data gathering method used, should be to obtain all the information necessary to identify the critical (essential) duties required, to fulfill the purpose of the position.

JOB FUNCTION DOCUMENTATION

On the worksheet, the essential or critical functions (duties and tasks) will be identified on the page entitled, **"Job Functions"**. The functions will be identified by action verbs used to describe the workers' action. This sentence structure is discussed in greater detail in Chapter 6. Each function can be quantified by the percentage of time spent performing it daily. Functions performed, other than daily, should not be quantified by a percentage of the "daily" time. These non-daily but critical functions may be quantified according to their performance, i.e., weekly, monthly, annually, required when needed, etc.

Indicate that a function is "critical" if the answer is "yes" to the question–**"Would the flow of work be interrupted by not performing the function?"** Remember, by definition, performance of a marginal duty would not be "critical" for job performance.

Example:

JOB FUNCTIONS

Essential Functions: Identify the critical duties actually performed by incumbents to fulfill the purpose of this position.

Write in prescribed sentence structure: action verb, object, [to] outcome, using M, E, T, W/A (machines, equipment, etc.).

Mark the "critical" box if not performing the duty would interrupt the flow of work. Include the daily % of time spent performing the critical duties. May not equal 100% due to performance of marginal duties.

DAILY % TIME	CRITICAL	ACTION VERB	OBJECT	[TO] OUTCOME/METW/A
10%	✔	Reads	Instructions	To complete the form
40%	✔	UNLOADS	MERCHANDISE	FROM INCOMING CONVEYANCES USING HANDCART, ETC.
20%	✔	VISUALLY VERIFIES	TYPE AND QUANTITY OF MERCHANDISE	WITH RECEIVING AND SHIPPING DOCUMENTATION
20%	✔	MARKS	IDENTIFICATION DETAILS	ONTO MERCHANDISE AND DOCUMENTATION USING WRITING UTENSILS AND TICKETS
20%	✔	SELECTS AND ARRANGES	STORED MERCHANDISE	ONTO CONVEYOR PER ESTABLISHED PROCEDURES

STEP FIVE—IDENTIFYING AND VERIFYING THE POSITION RELATED QUALIFICATIONS

If a position qualification document has been prepared, review the document with the participants. Request the participants' comment on the relevance of the qualifications to the critical functions of the position. Verify that the qualifications for performance of the functions are consistent with business necessity.

Many employers have not determined and documented relevant qualifications for specific position(s). When employers do identify qualifications they may include:

1. Level of education/training

2. Number of years of experience

3. Specific skills/abilities

4. Specific areas of knowledge

5. Required licenses and certifications

6. Insurability (bondable, driving record, etc.)

7. Employment eligibility (residency/citizenship)

The terms commonly used in qualification documents are:

- **Experience**—the amount of time previously spent performing specific duties or similar functions.

- **Skills/Abilities**—Acquired skills, competencies or proficiencies required to adequately perform the functions.

- **Knowledge**—information or facts known and required to be called upon to carry out the assigned functions.

- **Licenses/Certifications**—formal documentation verifying the attainment of some level of achievement or demonstrated abilities.

Completion of the **"Job Qualifications"** Section of the Job Analysis Worksheet will facilitate identification of the required qualifications necessary to carry out the purpose and critical functions of the position.

The job qualifications analyzed and documented on the worksheet are:

- Reasoning Ability

- Math and Language Development

- Educational Achievement

- Experience/Knowledge Desired

- License/Certification Desired

- Perceptual Aptitudes

- Worker-Skill Relationships to Data, People, Things

- Personal Traits

The Job Analyst will determine by interview and observation if the qualifications are required (present) or not required (not present) to fulfill the purpose of the position. The worksheet will facilitate the inquiry and documentation of those qualifications necessary in the position.

REASONING, MATH AND LANGUAGE DEVELOPMENT

Table 3–4 will assist the Analyst to better understand and evaluate each of the four categories of development.

Table 3–4

POSITION	PURPOSE
REASONING	The developmental level of a worker, per formal training or experience, to follow instructions or independently select the specific worker actions. In a specific position one or more than one level of reasoning may be required to carry out the critical functions.
MATHEMATICS	The level of achievement in performing arithmetic. The Selection of "simple" versus "complex" does not require performance of all the types of arithmetic in each category; in some positions no arithmetic may be required.
READING	The level of achievement distinguished by vocabulary and comprehension of the English language, unless otherwise documented. The selection of "simple" versus "complex" does not require performance of all the types of reading in each category; in some positions no reading may be required.
WRITING	The demonstrated level of achievement distinguished by vocabulary, spelling and use of the rules of grammar of the English language, unless otherwise documented. The selection of "simple" versus "complex" does not require performance of all the types of writing in each category; in some positions no writing may be required.

EDUCATIONAL ACHIEVEMENT

Identify the necessary level of education for the position. *Specify why the desired level of education is a business necessity to perform the critical duties of the position.*

EXPERIENCE/KNOWLEDGE DESIRED

Identify the specific type and duration of experience and/or knowledge desired. *Specify why the experience and/or knowledge is a business necessity to perform the critical duties of the position.*

LICENSE/CERTIFICATION DESIRED

List the required licenses and certificates. *Specify why the documents are a business necessity to perform the critical duties of this position.*

WORKER TRAITS DESIRED

The remaining Factors (5-9) require the Analyst to verify if the skill or trait is required (present) or not required (not present) to fulfill the purpose of the position. The items listed in Factors 5-8 are further defined in Appendix D.

Example:

The **"Job Qualifications"** section of the job analysis worksheet is completed on the next page for the warehouse worker position. This example illustrates the identification and verification of qualifications and related data collected in the interview of worker(s) and supervisors.

JOB QUALIFICATIONS

MENTAL FACTORS

FACTOR 1 — GENERAL EDUCATION DEVELOPMENT

REASONING

	PRESENT	NOT PRESENT
Deal with abstract and concrete variables, define problems, collect data, establish facts, and draw valid conclusions	☐	☒
Interpret instructions furnished in written, oral, diagrammatic, or schedule form	☐	☒
Deal with problems from standard situations	☐	☒
Carry out detailed but uninvolved written or oral instructions	☒	☐
Carry out single one or two step instructions	☒	☐

MATHEMATICS

	PRESENT	NOT PRESENT
COMPLEX SKILLS Business math, algebra, geometry, shopmath or statistics	☐	☒
SIMPLE SKILLS Add, subtract, multiply and divide whole numbers and fractions, make change, calculate time, calculate simple measurements	☒	☐

READING

	PRESENT	NOT PRESENT
COMPLEX SKILLS Comprehend newspapers, manuals, journals, instructions in use and maintenance of shop tools and equipment, safety rules and procedures and drawings	☐	☒
SIMPLE SKILLS English at the 6th grade level (tested), comprehend simple instructions or notations from a log book	☒	☐

FACTOR 1	GENERAL EDUCATION DEVELOPMENT	continued

WRITING   PRESENT   NOT PRESENT

COMPLEX SKILLS

Prepare business letters, summaries of reports using
prescribed format and conforming to all rules of spelling,
punctuation, grammar, diction and style .... ☐   ☒

SIMPLE SKILLS

English sentences containing subject, verb and object;
names and addresses, complete job application or
notations in a log book .... ☒   ☐

FACTOR 2	EDUCATIONAL ACHIEVEMENT

High School: ☒ Yes ☐ No

College Degree: ☐ Associate   ☐ Bachelor   ☐ Masters   ☐ Doctorate

Trade School: (Specify) _____

A HIGH SCHOOL DIPLOMA OR GED EQUIVALENCY IS ACCEPTABLE
VERIFICATION OF EDUCATIONAL ACHIEVEMENT.

FACTOR 3	EXPERIENCE/KNOWLEDGE DESIRED

(Specify type and duration) _MINIMUM EDUCATIONAL ACHIEVEMENT OR 6 MONTHS_
OF PROGRESSIVELY RESPONSIBLE GENERAL WORK EXPERIENCE MAINTAINING
RECORDS, SCREENING, REVIEWING, VERIFYING AND PREPARING DOCUMENTS.

FACTOR 4	LICENSE/CERTIFICATION

Valid Drivers License: ☐ Yes   ☒ No

Other: (Specify) _____

FACTOR 5	PERCEPTION

	PRESENT	NOT PRESENT
SPATIAL:	☐	☒

Ability to comprehend forms in space and understand relationships of plane and solid objects. May be used in such tasks as blueprint reading and in solving geometry problems. Frequently described as the ability to "visualize" objects of two or three dimensions, or to think visually of geometric forms.

	PRESENT	NOT PRESENT
FORM:	☒	☐

Ability to perceive pertinent detail in objects or in pictorial or graphic material. To make visual comparisons and discriminations and see slight differences in shapes and shadings of figures and widths and lengths of line.

	PRESENT	NOT PRESENT
CLERICAL:	☒	☐

Ability to perceive pertinent detail in verbal or tabular material. To observe differences in copy, to proof-read words and numbers, and to avoid perceptual errors in arithmetic computation.

FACTOR 6	DATA

Information, knowledge, and conceptions, related to data, people, or things, obtained by observation, and mental creation. Data is intangible and include numbers, words, symbols, ideas, concepts, and oral verbalization.

	PRESENT	NOT PRESENT
SYNTHESIZING	☐	☒
COORDINATING	☐	☒
ANALYZING	☐	☒
COMPILING	☐	☒
COMPUTING	☐	☒
COPYING	☐	☒
COMPARING.	☒	☐

FACTOR 7 — PEOPLE

Human beings; also animals dealt with on an individual basis as if they were human.

	PRESENT	NOT PRESENT
MENTORING	☐	☒
NEGOTIATING	☐	☒
INSTRUCTION	☐	☒
SUPERVISING	☐	☒
DIVERTING	☐	☒
PERSUADING	☐	☒
SPEAKING-SIGNALING	☐	☒
SERVING	☐	☒
TAKING INSTRUCTIONS-HELPING	☒	☐

FACTOR 8 — THINGS

Inanimate objects as distinguished from human beings, substances, or materials; machines, tools, equipment and products. A thing is tangible and has shape, form, and other physical characteristics.

	PRESENT	NOT PRESENT
SETTING UP	☐	☒
PRECISION WORKING	☐	☒
OPERATING-CONTROLLING	☐	☒
DRIVING-OPERATION	☐	☒
MANIPULATING	☐	☒
TENDING	☒	☐
FEEDING-OFFBEARING	☒	☐
HANDLING	☒	☐

ADA–Essential Function Identification

FACTOR 9	PERSONAL TRAITS

Work functions required by specific job-worker situations.

	PRESENT	**NOT PRESENT**

I. ABILITY TO COMPREHEND AND FOLLOW INSTRUCTIONS .... ☒   ❑

The ability to maintain attention and concentration for necessary periods; to apply common sense understanding to carry out instructions furnished in written, oral or diagrammatic form; to adapt to situations requiring the precise attainment of set limits, tolerances or standards; to operate–controls which involve starting, stopping, controlling and adjusting the progress of a machine or piece of equipment.

II. ABILITY TO PERFORM SIMPLE AND REPETITIVE TASKS .... ☒   ❑

The ability to ask simple questions or request assistance; to perform activities of a routine, concrete, organized nature; to remember locations and work procedures; to make decisions based on simple sensory data.

III. ABILITY TO MAINTAIN A WORK PACE APPROPRIATE TO A GIVEN WORK LOAD .... ☒   ❑

The ability to perform activities with a schedule, maintain regular attendance and to be punctual within specified tolerances; to complete a normal work day and/or work week and perform at a consistent pace without unreasonable number and/or length of rest periods; to perform effectively when confronted with potential emergency, critical, unusual or dangerous situations, or in situations in which working speed and sustained attention are make or break aspects of the job (i.e., police work, fire fighter, life guard, crossing guard, security guard, bouncer, body guard, paramedic, emergency room personnel, ICU/CCU nurse, etc.).

IV. ABILITY TO RELATE TO OTHER PEOPLE BEYOND GIVING AND RECEIVING INSTRUCTIONS .... ❑   ☒

The ability to get along with co–workers or peers without exhibiting extreme responses; to perform work activities requiring negotiating with, instructing, supervising, persuading or speaking; to respond appropriately to criticism from a supervisor.

V. ABILITY TO INFLUENCE PEOPLE .... ❑   ☒

The ability to convince or redirect others; to understand the meanings of words and to use them effectively; to interact appropriately with the general public.

VI. ABILITY TO PERFORM COMPLEX OR VARIED TASKS .... ❑   ☒

The ability to synthesize, coordinate and analyze data; to perform jobs requiring precise attainment of set limits, tolerances or standards.

VII. ABILITY TO MAKE GENERALIZATIONS, EVALUATIONS OR DECISIONS WITHOUT IMMEDIATE SUPERVISION .... ❑   ☒

The ability to retain awareness of potential hazards and observe appropriate precautions; to understand and remember detailed instructions; to travel in unfamiliar places or use public transportation systems.

VIII. ABILITY TO ACCEPT AND CARRY OUT RESPONSIBILITY FOR DIRECTION, CONTROL AND PLANNING .... ❑   ☒

The ability to set realistic goals or make plans independently of others; to negotiate with, instruct or supervise people; to respond appropriately to changes in the work setting.

SUMMARY

The Interview—Observation methodology is widely accepted and highly recommended for conducting job analyses in industry. In this chapter, interviewing techniques were reviewed. To review, the five key steps to a successful interview are listed in Table 3–5.

Steps	Description
STEP ONE	Arranging and Commencement of the Interview
Step Two	Gathering Preliminary Information
Step Three	Clarification of the Purpose of the Position
Step Four	Identifying the Functions (Duties and Tasks)
Step Five	Identification of Position Related Qualifications

Table 3–5

A job analysis interview worksheet is critical for documenting the interview data. The worksheet identifies the data to gather, organizes the collected data, and provides an inclusive format for data collection. An **"Essential Functions - Demands Job Analysis Worksheet"** was described. It was used as an example to illustrate how to complete an interview worksheet during an on-site interview.

The interview is only one third of the job analysis methodology discussed in this book. Chapter 4 will describe how and what to observe to document and quantify the physical demands and environmental factors of work. Chapter 5 will guide the Analyst through the specific procedures of identifying and verifying the essential functions per ADA. In Chapter 6, the last third of the methodology, report writing guidelines, are explained.

Now that Mr. Watson has completed the training in interviewing techniques, he will continue the training in observation techniques in Chapter 4.

CHAPTER 4

DATA GATHERING PROCEDURES— OBSERVATION TECHNIQUES

Techniques for conducting data gathering interviews to qualify and quantify essential functions and establish complete position requirements.

OBSERVATION MODEL

*Per Webster's New World Dictionary, the definition of **analysis** is,*

"1. A separating or breaking up of any whole into its parts, especially with an examination of these parts to find out their nature, proportion, function, interrelationship, etc. 2. A statement of the results of this process."

Job analysis is the breaking up of a position into its parts to examine by observing each of these parts. The parts observed include duties and tasks; environmental conditions; use of machines, equipment, tools and work aids; and physical demands.

As discussed in Chapter 3, in addition to interviewing knowledgeable individuals to analyze a position, it is necessary to observe the position. Observation is the method in which the separate parts of the position can be examined and evaluated first hand. The Analyst may decide to either observe the work simultaneously with receiving explanation or to obtain an explanation and then observe the work. This is a decision of the Analyst. However, the job analysis must include first hand observation to obtain the best understanding of the position and to quantify, qualify and evaluate its' parts.

In this chapter the Analyst will learn observation techniques to analyze the individual functions and requirements of positions.

The requirements of positions are primarily comprised of the physical demands. The physical demands include: the mobility requirements, vertical work requirements, horizontal work requirements, strength and agility requirements. The machines, equipment, tools and work aids utilized by the worker to physically carry out the functions are important to identify and evaluate. The environmental conditions encountered by the worker when performing the assigned duties and tasks are also important to identify.

The following is a detailed discussion of the five components of the observation model.

FUNCTION VERIFICATION

The **first component** of the on-site observation is to verify that the duties and tasks as identified in the interview portion of the process are actually performed in the position being analyzed. The common work areas where the normal performance of the duties takes place must be verified. The Analyst should obtain a clear understanding of the flow of the work going into and out of the workstation(s) being analyzed, and identify the relationship of the position being analyzed to other positions in the department.

Qualifying Functions

The **second component** of observation is to qualify as objectively as possible the various functional components of the position. Qualifying includes; **timing** the time spent performing the functions using a stop watch, and actually **counting** the cycles or repetitions of functions being performed; **measuring** the physical demands and actually **weighing** objects handled to determine the strength/force requirements.

Quantifying Functions

The **third component** of observation is to objectively quantify the requirements of the position. Analyst's tools and equipment used to quantify the physical requirements include:

- Portable scale
- Stop watch
- Angle finder

- Push and pull gauges
- Measuring tape
- Calculator

Quantifying gives dimension to the various functions being performed. Measurements are labeled in the forms of:

MEASUREMENTS	DESCRIPTION
Repetitions	The number of times the same activity is completed.
Frequency	The amount of time the same activity occurs within a specified interval.
Duration	The single continuous length of time of an activity.
Distance	A measured horizontal length.
Height	A measured vertical length.
Size	The overall dimensions of an object.
Amount	A total sum or quantity of something.
Weight	A measure of the heaviness of objects.
Cycle Time	A single complete execution of an expected sequence of activities.

Table 4–1

A common Categorical measure of frequency is; occasional, frequent and continuous. The **Revised Handbook for Analyzing Jobs** has defined these terms as follows:

FREQUENCY	DESCRIPTION
Occasional	Up to 1/3 of work shift (For an 8 hour work shift - up to 3 hours)
Frequent	1/3 to 2/3's of work shift (For an 8 hour work shift - 3 to 5 hours)
Continuous	More than 2/3's of work shift (For an 8 hour work shift - 5 to 8 hours)

Table 4-2

PHOTOGRAPHY

The **fourth component** in the observation of positions is to photograph various tasks for later analysis of the physical components. A 35mm or Polaroid camera or video CamCorder may be utilized to perform the photography.

For best results, the camera should be equipped with either a 28mm lens or telephoto (55mm to 28mm) lens. The wide angle lens will permit photography within close proximity of the work being observed. Usually photos are taken within 10' of the actual work being observed. The camera should be equipped with a flash as most industrial settings are dimly lit.

Photography may be used to enhance the reader's understanding of the position description. The physical components of the position, unusual machinery or equipment used or unusual tasks which are difficult to explain may be better understood with a visual display.

Video CamCorders are beneficial for photographing functions which are not easily photographed with 35mm photography. For example, positions with repetitive cycles, upper extremity repetitive motions and rapid motion activities are better understood and analyzed by video photography.

Physical Demands Identification

The **fifth component** of the observation model is identifying the physical demands. The physical demands of each position are comprised of five categories of physical functioning. Those categories are:

- Mobility
- Vertical work
- Horizontal work
- Strength requirements
- Agilities

The worker normally physically performs in a position using a combination of these functions. Each of these categories must be analyzed to compare, contrast and document the physical functions individually and their interrelationships.

Mobility

The mobility requirements of the position need to be quantified. The category–Mobility normally includes the walking, standing and sitting required to carry out the job duties. (In some positions, running would also be a factor of mobility).

As illustrated in Figure 4–1 there is a relationship between the Data, People, and Thing traits and the mobility requirements of a position.

DATA, PEOPLE, THINGS VS. MOBILITY

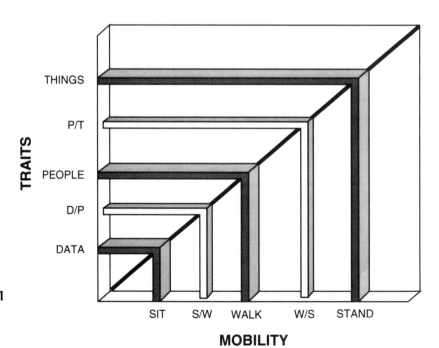

Figure 4–1

As illustrated in Figure 4–1, those positions that are primarily sitting would have more involvement with data, with some exceptions of small assembly or inspection type duties.

Examples of "Data" Jobs are:

In contrast those positions requiring more involvement with things generally have more standing or standing/walking activities required to carry out the job duties.

Examples of "Things" Jobs are:

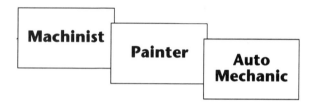

Positions requiring involvement with people generally have combinations of sitting, walking and standing depending on the type of people involvement required in the position.

Examples of "People" Jobs are:

In order to establish the percentage (%) of time spent standing, walking or sitting the Analyst could ask these questions of the interviewees:

Q: If your 8 hour work day equals 100% not counting breaks and lunch, what percent of the time are you on your feet versus off your feet?

A: (The worker can typically apply a percentage to on/off of feet.)

Q: During the percentage of time you are off your feet, are you sitting at a desk, on a stool or driving a vehicle?

A: (The worker can usually clarify the sitting conditions very easily)

Q: Of the percentage of time you are on your feet, what percent are you stationary and what percent are you on the move (walking)?

A: (The worker can usually apply a percentage to being stationary or moving)

Q: Therefore, of an 8 hour work day you spend approximately,

$$\underline{\quad X \quad} \text{ \% of time sitting?}$$
$$\underline{\quad Y \quad} \text{ \% of time standing?}$$
$$\underline{\quad Z \quad} \text{ \% of time walking?}$$
$$100 \text{ \%}$$

A: (Obtain verification or clarification to this summary of mobility)

Q: What duties are you performing while you are:

Sitting?

Standing?

Walking?

A: (The worker's response should be a reasonable match with the information provided during the previous interview of job functions)

Q: Clarify any discrepancies. Ask the supervisor for verification of the mobility requirements.

It is most important that the job analysis not continue until mobility is quantified and verified at the job site by interview and observation.

The relationship of mobility to Data, People, Things is another objective measure used to quantify mobility. For example, the Analyst can assume that a Data type occupation is most likely performed in a sitting position. Conversely, a sitting position is more likely to have mostly Data functions. This is only a rule of thumb for the Analyst to use as a measure of functions, not as an absolute fact.

The first page of the **"Job Requirement"** Section of the Job Analysis Worksheet, **Factor 1 Strength**. The first category is **Mobility**. Complete the form by determining the percentage per work day, the number of hours per work day or the frequency category to specify the mobility requirements. (Refer to Chapter 3).

Example:

JOB REQUIREMENTS

PHYSICAL FACTORS

KEY:	NP	=	Not Present	O	=	1/3 of the day
	F	=	1/3–2/3 of the day	C	=	Over 2/3 of the day

FACTOR 1: STRENGTH

MOBILITY   **FREQUENCY**

					NP	O	F	C
A.	Stand	_45_ % of time	_35_ hrs/day		☐	☐	☒	☐
B.	Walk	_55_ % of time	_45_ hrs/day		☐	☐	☒	☐
C.	Sit	_0_ % of time	_0_ hrs/day		☒	☐	☐	☐
		100%	4(8)10 hrs/day					

COMMENTS: _WALKS UPON CONCRETE LEVEL SURFACE IN WAREHOUSE, STANDS ON RUBBER MAT AT CONVEYOR AND MACHINES._

VERTICAL WORK AREAS

Only after determining and verifying the mobility requirements of the position, can the work in the horizontal and vertical planes be identified. For example, a position requiring more walking generally will have greater amounts of work in the horizontal plane than a standing position. Seated workstations, primarily desk work, bench work, or driving positions, are work tasks performed in the vertical plane.

The vertical work area of a position is limited by an individual's height and reach with their arms. If the dimensions of the vertical work area are from the feet or the surface on which the person is standing, to the height in which their hand will reach overhead, we call this the vertical work plane. As illustrated in Figure 4–2, this plane can be divided into three sections: the area below knee level or up to approximately 20"; the area between 20" to 54" or chest level, and the area above the chest or approximately 54" from the floor.

VERTICAL PLANE

One Dimensional

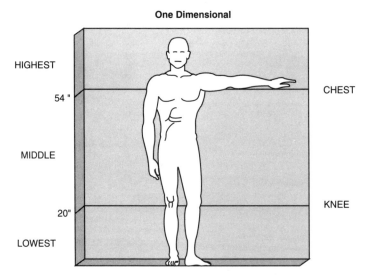

HIGHEST

54"

MIDDLE

20"

LOWEST

CHEST

KNEE

Figure 4–2

In consideration of the following Anthropometric Model (Figure 4–3), an individual's height in inches, and the lengths between the various joints of an individual can be calculated and used as a measuring device.

Anthropometric Model

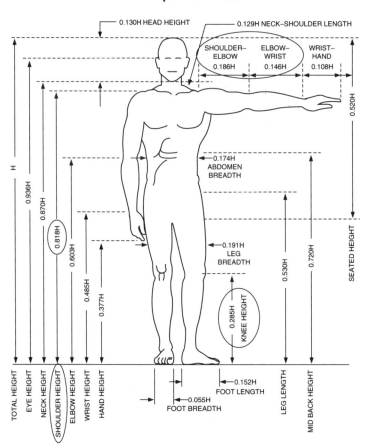

Figure 4–3

Using the Anthropometric Model, calculate the distance between the floor and your knee height, shoulder height and the length of your arm. Locate the desired measurement and multiply the proportionate factor of height (H) times your height (in inches). These three are the most useful dimensions for the Analyst to have calculated. The formulas are:

Your height in inches = H

H x .285   =   Knee height

H x .818   =   Shoulder height
(Chest approximately 6" below shoulder)

H x .332   =   Arm length

For example, if you are 5'10" tall your height (H) is:

5'	x	12"	=	60"
60"	+	10"	=	70"
	H		=	70"

Knee Height	=	70" (H)	x	.285
Knee Height	=	19.95" (or 20")		
Shoulder Height	=	70" (H)	x	.818
Shoulder Height	=	57.26" (or 57")		
Chest Height	=	51" (57"–6")		
Arm Length	=	70" (H)	x	.332
Arm Length	=	23.24" (or 23")		

Now you are a human measuring instrument. When you walk into a work setting, you can immediately begin to observe for functions being performed in the lowest work area (below knee height), middle work area (between knee and chest height), and highest work area (above chest height).

As illustrated in Figure 4–4, on the bell curves below, 90 percent of female heights range between 59.9" and 67.7" and 90 percent of male heights range between 64.4" and 73.0".

Assuming these studies are accurate, do you fall within the "normal" range of the 90% group by gender? If you do not, you must consider your size in comparison of the population typically hired by an employer for specific position(s) before using your body segments to measure and make assumptions about the relationship of the work area to individual employees.

Normal Frequency Distribution

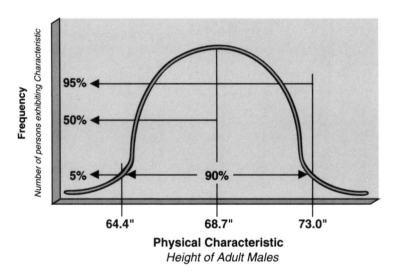

Physical Characteristic
Height of Adult Males

Figure 4–4

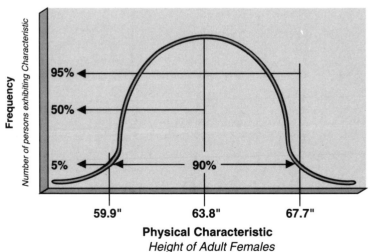

Physical Characteristic
Height of Adult Females

The vertical work plane is illustrated in Figure 4–5. The three vertical work areas are defined by a worker's knees and chest height.

PHYSICAL AGILITIES VS. MOBILITY

Two Dimensional

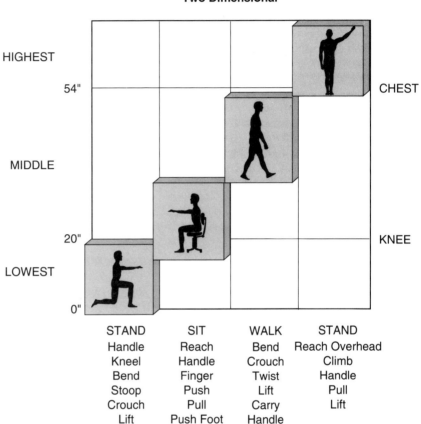

Figure 4–5

STAND	SIT	WALK	STAND
Handle	Reach	Bend	Reach Overhead
Kneel	Handle	Crouch	Climb
Bend	Finger	Twist	Handle
Stoop	Push	Lift	Pull
Crouch	Pull	Carry	Lift
Lift	Push Foot	Handle	
Crawl	Pedal	Push	
Lay		Pull	
Push Foot			
Pedal			

In stationary work where the individual would be standing or otherwise positioned stationary the physical functions can be easily determined. For example; in the lowest area of the vertical plane, below knee height, the individual may perform:

- Kneeling
- Crouching
- Stooping
- Crawling
- Laying

As an accommodation, the use of tools or work implements may be utilized to perform work in the lowest area to minimize the need for crouching or kneeling. Examples would be use of broom and mop to clean floor rather than using rags on hands and knees. Or, to dig a trench using shovel rather than on hands and knees.

Conversely, stationary work in the highest area of the vertical plane, above chest height, would require the individual to perform overhead reaching or climbing ladders to elevate up to the necessary work height. Tools or work implements can be used as an accommodation to perform work above head height and minimize the need to reach or climb. Examples would be to pull a rope or chain to lower or raise an overhead door, and/or to use an extension stick to elevate paint rollers.

Most workstations, regardless of the mobility requirement, are designed to perform work primarily in the middle area of the vertical plane. Most of the physical functions of bending, twisting, reaching (forward flexion/abduction), lifting, carrying, pushing and pulling are performed between knee and chest height. See Figure 4–5.

Work performed primarily in the vertical plane more frequently requires flexibility of the low back and lower extremities. Examples of occupations performed in the vertical work area include:

- Construction Worker
- Mail Carrier
- Welder
- Laborer
- Machinist
- Electrician

Horizontal Work Area

The horizontal work area is defined by the arm length of a worker. The worker may be in a seated or standing position. The seated position generally finds the individual working in a horizontal plane within the distance from the elbow to the hand. (Approximately 15") Whereas the individual standing will generally work horizontally within the dimensions from the body to the full extension of the arm. (Approximately 30") To work horizontally beyond the extension of the arm requires the individual to either walk to reposition self or to use tools or work implements. Figure 4–6 illustrates the seated worker in relationship to the vertical work plane.

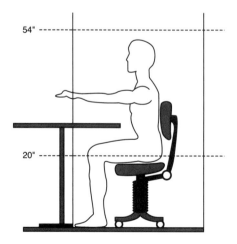

Figure 4–6

Figure 4–7 illustrates the seated or standing worker in relationship to the horizontal work plane.

Figure 4–7

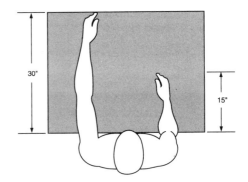

Figures 4–8 and 4–9 illustrates how to calculate the seated or standing work position in relation to the horizontal work area.

Figure 4–8

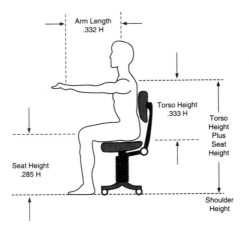

Figure 4–9

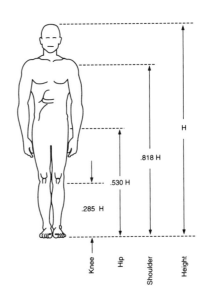

The horizontal work area workstations are designed to perform functions with the upper extremities in a stationary standing or seated posture.

Examples of occupations performed in the horizontal work area include:

- Typist
- Secretary
- Receptionist
- Computer Programmer
- Manager
- Production Assembler

Strength

The strength requirements of a position are generally defined by the lifting (vertical distance), carrying (horizontal distance), and pushing and pulling forces required. In discussing the strength requirements, the qualification and quantifying of these activities are most important. Another objective measure of strength is the relationship of mobility to the expected lifting and carrying forces exerted.

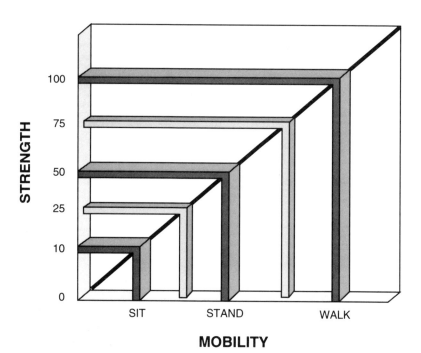

Figure 4–10

As illustrated in Figure 4–10, seated positions most frequently require substantially less strength demands than walking positions. Walking positions generally require the greatest amount of strength demand.

On the job analysis worksheet, after the first category, **Mobility,** the second category under **Strength** is **"Lifting"**. Lifting is the relocating of an object, a vertical distance between the worker's feet and overhead reach. On the Worksheet, the weight categories are identified and a category of **"FREQUENCY"** is determined to represent the range of lifting performed. Brief comments are prepared to identify the heaviest objects and the vertical distances handled. These quantifications should be obtained by use of a portable scale to actually measure weight, and a tape measure to measure actual distances.

Example:

LIFTING		FREQUENCY		
	NP	O	F	C
up to 5 lbs	☐	☐	☒	☐
6 - 10 lbs	☐	☐	☒	☐
11 - 20 lbs	☐	☐	☒	☐
21 - 25 lbs	☐	☐	☒	☐
26 - 50 lbs	☐	☒	☐	☐
51 - 75 lbs	☐	☒	☐	☐
76 - 100 lbs	☒	☐	☐	☐
Over 100 lbs	☒	☐	☐	☐

COMMENTS: (Heaviest item and range of vertical distance) _SURFACE FREIGHT CARTONS MAY WEIGH A MAXIMUM OF 70 POUNDS. MOST CARTONS HANDLED WEIGH LESS THAN 30 POUNDS. THE CARTONS ARE LIFTED A MAXIMUM OF 35" ONTO OR OFF OF CONVEYOR FROM/TO WAREHOUSE PALLET ON FLOOR._

A word of caution to the Analyst, it should not be determined that it is essential that the warehouse worker be able to manually lift up to 70 pounds. This represents only the customary manner and means. This is an example of a function where a reasonable accommodation may be considered for a qualified individual with a disability. The essential function is to load cartons onto/off of the conveyor. If the disability was, "no repetitive bending", then an accommodation maybe to raise the warehouse pallet up off of the floor with a forklift, to permit loading the cartons onto the conveyor without bending. Or, perhaps the warehouse pallet could be staged onto a platform next to the conveyors, to minimize the bending required to load cartons onto/off of the conveyor.

The third category of **Strength** is **"Carrying"**. This is relocating an object a horizontal distance. (From point A to point B). The objects carried are weighed at the job site using a portable scale. The frequency and distance they are carried are calculated. The category representing the weight is identified and the frequency for carrying objects of that weight is documented. For a wide range of objects carried, the frequency for each category of weight should be determined. Examples of the heaviest items carried and the range of distance carried should be entered in the comment section of the Job Analysis Worksheet.

Example:

FACTOR 1:	STRENGTH				Continued
CARRYING				**FREQUENCY**	

	NP	**O**	**F**	**C**
up to 5 lbs	❑	❑	❑	☒
6 - 10 lbs	❑	❑	❑	☒
11 - 20 lbs...	❑	❑	☒	❑
21 - 25 lbs	❑	☒	❑	❑
26 - 50 lbs	☒	❑	❑	❑
51 - 75 lbs	☒	❑	❑	❑
76 - 100 lbs	☒	❑	❑	❑
Over 100 lbs	☒	❑	❑	❑

COMMENTS: (Heaviest item and range of horizontal distance) *INFREQUENTLY A CARTON WEIGHING UP TO 50 POUNDS IS CARRIED 40', THE LENGTH OF A SHIPPING CONTAINER. MOST CARTONS ARE CARRIED LESS THAN 15 FEET AND WEIGH LESS THAN 30 POUNDS.*

Much like lifting, it should not be determined essential, or that carrying up to 50 pounds for forty feet is required, based on the reported customary methods observed. The essential function is to occasionally transport cartons weighing 30 to 50 pounds a maximum of 40". Again, a reasonable accommodation for Mr. Williams may be to provide a two wheel dolly, pallet jack or forklift to transport the heavy cartons.

The fourth category of **Strength** is **"Pushing and Pulling"**. This is a physical effort extended upon an object to cause it to move. The static strength required to cause the object to move can be measured in "pounds" with push and pull gauges. If weight categories are going to be selected, then it is paramount that these strengths be measured. Note, the weight of the object being moved is not the static strength measurement, or the push/pull weight measurement.

If the static strength is not going to be measured, an alternative, to quantifying the static strength, is to describe the conditions of the pushing and pulling tasks.

For example, use concise sentences to describe the footwear and surfaces walked upon while pushing/pulling. Describe wheel diameters and type, describe and list specific items being pushed/pulled, measure angle of surfaces, measure and document the duration, weight and/or height of items pushed/pulled, discuss pushing on foot pedals and hand controls, discuss pushing and pulling on hand tools and equipment to use, discuss use of unilateral vs bilateral foot and arm use. Be as specific in the description as possible of the conditions of the push/pull activity.

Example:

PUSHING/PULLING	FREQUENCY			
	NP	O	F	C
5 lbs	☐	☐	☒	☐
6 - 10 lbs	☐	☐	☒	☐
11 - 20 lbs	☐	☐	☒	☐
21 - 25 lbs	☒	☐	☐	☐
26 - 50 lbs	☒	☐	☐	☐
51 - 75 lbs	☒	☐	☐	☐
76 - 100 lbs	☒	☐	☐	☐.
Over 100 lbs	☒	☐	☐	☐

COMMENTS: (Wheeled objects, Footpedal, Lever, Equipment or Hand tool) _USES PUSH/PULL MOTION TO MANUALLY MOVE CARTONS ON ROLLERS OF CONVEYORS SYSTEM._

AGILITIES

The physical activities identified in Factors 2-7 are:

- **Agility**
- **Dexterity**
- **Coordination**
- **Vision**
- **Talking**
- **Hearing**

These activities can be observed and verified by interview of the workers. The individual activities are identified and categorized according to the frequency with which they are required to carry out the purpose of the position.

Example:

FACTOR 2:		AGILITY				Continued

FREQUENCY

		NP	O	F	C
G.	Crawling	☒	❏	❏	❏
H.	Running	☒	❏	❏	❏
I.	Twisting	❏	☒	❏	❏
J.	Turning	❏	☒	❏	❏
K.	Jumping	☒	❏	❏	❏

COMMENTS: _____

_____

_____

FACTOR 3:		DEXTERITY			

FREQUENCY

		NP	O	F	C
A.	Grasping–Firm/Strong	❏	❏	☒	❏
B.	Finger Dexterity	❏	❏	☒	❏
C.	Reaching Forward	❏	❏	☒	❏
D.	Reaching Overhead	❏	☒	❏	❏
E.	Pinching	❏	☒	❏	❏
F.	Grasping–Light	❏	☒	❏	❏

Dominant hand: ☒ Right ❏ Left ❏ Both

COMMENTS: _____

_____

_____

FACTOR 4:		COORDINATION			

FREQUENCY

		NP	O	F	C
A.	Eye - hand	❏	❏	❏	☒
B.	Eye - Hand - Foot	☒	❏	❏	❏
C.	Driving	☒	❏	❏	❏

COMMENTS: _____

_____

_____

FACTOR 5: VISION

FREQUENCY

		NP	O	F	C
A.	Acuity, Near	☐	☐	☐	☒
B.	Acuity, Far	☐	☐	☐	☒
C.	Depth Perception	☒	☐	☐	☐
D.	Accommodation	☒	☐	☐	☐
E.	Color Vision	☐	☒	☐	☐
F.	Field of Vision	☒	☐	☐	☐

COMMENTS: _____

_____

_____

FACTOR 6: TALKING

FREQUENCY

		NP	O	F	C
A.	Face-to-Face Contact	☐	☐	☒	☐
B.	Verbal Contact with Others	☐	☒	☐	☐
C.	Public	☐	☒	☐	☐

COMMENTS: *PRIMARILY CONVERSES WITH CO-WORKERS, TRUCK DRIVERS AND SUPERVISOR. OCCASIONALLY ANSWERS THE TELEPHONE. OCCASIONALLY PROVIDES GENERAL INFORMATION TO A CUSTOMER.*

FACTOR 7: HEARING

FREQUENCY

		NP	O	F	C
A.	Normal Conversation	☐	☐	☐	☒
B.	Telephone Communication	☐	☒	☐	☐
C.	Earplugs Required	☒	☐	☐	☐

COMMENTS: _____

_____

_____

ENVIRONMENTAL CONDITIONS

It is necessary to identify the physical surroundings in which the worker performs the specific duties of their position. The U. S. Department of Labor has defined and categorized environmental conditions which can be used as benchmark terminology for analyzing positions. These conditions include:

1. Exposure to weather (inside, outside)

2. Extreme cold (non-weather related)

3. Extreme heat (non-weather related)

4. Wet and/or humid

5. Noise intensity level

6. Vibration

7. Atmospheric conditions (fumes, odors, toxic conditions, dust and poor ventilation)

8. Proximity to moving mechanical parts

9. Exposure to electrical shock

10. Working in high exposed places

11. Exposure to radiation

12. Working with explosives

13. Exposure to toxic or caustic chemicals

14. Other environmental conditions

These categories are defined in more detail in Appendix D.

Through my experience, I have identified additional environmental conditions, not defined by the U.S. Department of Labor, that are important considerations of the work environment. For example, the **lighting** of the work area and the type of lighting which is available is an important environmental consideration. It is important to indicate if while working at a desk, the workstation is illuminated by ceiling fluorescent lighting, and/or with additional desktop table lighting. If working outdoors, consider whether the worker works by sunlight or is there portable lighting set up or hand held.

Of equal importance, identify the **surfaces** the worker walks upon. Are the surfaces level, sloped, unlandscaped, landscaped, asphalt, gravel, dirt, concrete, wooden, carpeted, etc.?

When describing the various **exposures** to the worker, it is import-ant to be specific. For example in discussing **noise** it would be important to identify the source of the noise and the duration in which the worker may be exposed. A sound pressure level meter could be used to identify the specific decibels in which the worker is exposed. The U.S. Department of Labor categorizes levels of noise as:

1. Very Quiet (Forest Trail)

2. Quiet (Library)

3. Moderate (Light Traffic)

4. Loud (Heavy Traffic)

5. Very Loud (Jack Hammer Work)

In my experience, while in the work place, if I am unable to have a normal conversation at a normal distance from another individual I am interviewing, then I consider the possibility that ear protection may be required. I inquire as to the source and duration of the noise, and to the employer's requirement for ear protection (it may or may not be required by OSHA).

Also, if the employer requires particular **safety equipment** and/or clothing to be worn in the course of work this should be identified and documented. Examples would include, safety glasses, hard hats, ear plugs, hard toed shoes, uniforms, etc. Document them on the worksheet.

A helpful hint to remember is always request **Material Safety Data Sheets (MSDS)** to identify the hazards, ingredients, first aid and safety recommendations for chemicals, gases, aerosols, liquids, and fumes identified in the work place. Document on the worksheet that the MSDS are available and current. It is a good idea to request this information when the onsite appointment is confirmed.

The "Environmental Factors" are observed at the job site. The duration and frequency of exposure can be verified by interview of the workers. On the Job Analysis Worksheet, under Job Requirements, Environmental Factors are identified on the job and the frequency of exposure is notated.

For the warehouse worker, the exposures and safety factors are as follows:

Example:

ENVIRONMENTAL FACTORS

FREQUENCY

		NP	O	F	C
A.	Works indoors	❑	❑	❑	☒
B.	Works outdoors	☒	❑	❑	❑
C.	Exposure to extreme hot or cold temperature	☒	❑	❑	❑
D.	Working at unprotected heights	☒	❑	❑	❑
E.	Being around moving machinery	❑	❑	☒	❑
F.	Exposure to marked changes in temperature/humidity	❑	❑	☒	❑
G.	Exposure to dust, fumes, smoke, gases, odors, mists or other irritating particles (specify) _____	❑	❑	☒	❑
H.	Exposure to toxic or caustic chemicals	☒	❑	❑	❑
I.	Exposure to excessive noises	☒	❑	❑	❑
J.	Exposure to radiation or electrical energy	☒	❑	❑	❑
K.	Exposure to solvents, grease, or oils	☒	❑	❑	❑
L.	Exposure to slippery or uneven walking surfaces	❑	☒	❑	❑
M.	Working below ground	☒	❑	❑	❑
N.	Using computer (CRT) monitor	☒	❑	❑	❑
O.	Working with explosives	☒	❑	❑	❑
P.	Exposure to vibration	☒	❑	❑	❑
Q.	Exposure to flames or burning items	☒	❑	❑	❑
R.	Works around others	❑	❑	❑	☒
S.	Works alone	☒	❑	❑	❑
T.	Works with others	❑	❑	☒	❑

COMMENTS: (Describe special conditions) _____
_____
_____

SAFETY FACTORS

	PRESENT	NOT PRESENT
Material Safety Data Sheets (Verify Availability and Current)	☒	❑
Safety Equipment (Required to Wear)		
Safety Glasses	❑	☒
Ear Plugs	❑	☒
Hard Hat	❑	☒
Protective Clothing	❑	☒
Other _____	❑	☒
_____	❑	❑

MACHINES, EQUIPMENT, TOOLS AND WORK AIDS

It is important that the Analyst identify the machines, equipment, tools and work aids used by the worker for performing the various duties. These can be documented on the Job Analysis Worksheet. Identify on the worksheet if the use and operation of the machines, equipment, tools or work aids can be learned on the job (OJT) or if previous experience and knowledge is required (skilled).

It is common for there to be confusion in understanding the difference between machines, equipment, tools and work aids. The following definitions will assist the Analyst in differentiating by definition between these devices.

MACHINES

Machines are devices which are a combination of mechanical parts with a framework and fastenings to support and connect them. Machines are designed to apply force to do work on or move materials or to process data. Machines may be activated by hand and foot power applied through levers or buttons, or by any outside power source such as electricity, steam, hydraulics or compressed air. Generally machinery is something that cannot be picked up and moved by the worker. Vehicles are also examples of machinery. Machinery includes, printing presses, drill presses, lathes, conveyors, trucks, forklifts, copy machines, etc.

EQUIPMENT

Equipment includes devices which generally have power, communicate signals, or have an effect upon material through the application of light, heat, electric, compressed air, chemicals or atmospheric pressure. Equipment can be differentiated from machinery primarily in that they are able to be picked up, moved or transported to carry out the prescribed work. Examples of equipment include skilsaw, impact wrench, camera, two-way radio, drill motor, etc.

TOOLS

Tools are implements which are manipulated to do work and/or move materials. Tools are generally those objects which are not power actuated but are actuated by use. Tools include hand tools such as ratchets, wrenches, hammers, screwdrivers, pliers, etc. Tools may also be ladders, wheelbarrows, shovels, brooms, etc.

WORK AIDS

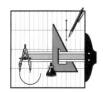

Work aids are miscellaneous items which cannot be considered machines, tools or equipment and yet are necessary for carrying out the duties. Examples include, blueprints, wiring diagrams, manuals, tape, writing utensils and drop cloths.

Example:

MACHINES • EQUIPMENT • TOOLS • WORK AIDS

MACHINES

Devices which are a combination of mechanical parts, power actuated and designed to apply force to do work on or move materials or to process data. Vehicles are considered to be machines.

LIST	SKILLED	OJT
NONE	☐	☐
	☐	☐
	☐	☐
	☐	☐
	☐	☐
	☐	☐
	☐	☐
	☐	☐
	☐	☐
	☐	☐

EQUIPMENT

Devices which are power actuated and generally designed to be portable and used to apply a force to do work on or move material or to process data.

LIST	SKILLED	OJT
TICKET MACHINE	☐	☒
CONVEYOR ROLLERS, PERMANENT	☒	☐
	☐	☐
	☐	☐
	☐	☐
	☐	☐
	☐	☐
	☐	☐
	☐	☐
	☐	☐

MACHINES • EQUIPMENT • TOOLS • WORK AIDS

TOOLS

Devices or implements which are not power actuated and are manipulated by hand to do work on or move materials.

LIST	SKILLED	OJT
PALLET JACK	☒	☐
HAND TRUCK	☒	☐
CARTS	☒	☐
TAPER	☐	☒
	☐	☐
	☐	☐
	☐	☐
	☐	☐
	☐	☐
	☐	☐

WORK AIDS

Items not considered to be a machine, equipment or tool yet are necessary for carrying out the work.

LIST	SKILLED	OJT
LADDER	☒	☐
WRITING UTENSILS	☒	☐
MARKING UTENSILS	☒	☐
STAPLER	☒	☐
	☐	☐
	☐	☐
	☐	☐
	☐	☐
	☐	☐
	☐	☐

KEY

OJT– The worker will need to learn to use upon commencing work in the position

SKILLED– The worker would need to have experience prior to commencing work in the position

SUMMARY:

Observation of workers performing work tasks is essential for objective qualification and quantification of individual's position functions, requirements and environmental conditions.

In this Chapter, an Observation Model was discussed in detail. The five components of the Observation Model are:

1. Function Verification

2. Qualifying Functions

3. Quantifying Functions

4. Photography

5. Physical Demand Identification

The author recommends, whenever possible, the analyst to have gathered all of the function (duty/task) data prior to observation of work functions. In this way the analyst will be more assured that the qualifying, quantifying and photography will be restricted to the position being analyzed. Qualifying and quantifying functions are completed by timing with a stopwatch, counting cycles or repetitions, measuring with a tape measure, and weighing with a scale. Photography is another form of objective evaluation of functions.

The fifth component of the Observation Model is physical demand identification. Five categories of physical functioning was discussed. These categories are:

1. Mobility

2. Vertical Work

3. Horizontal Work

4. Strength Requirements

5. Agility

The author suggests, that if the analyst knows the **height** of the worker(s) and can verify the **mobility** requirements of a position being analyzed, then through observation the analyst can:

1. Verify Functions

2. Assume Strength requirements

3. Identify and Quantify frequency of performing various physical agilities.

In this Chapter, an Anthropometric Model was provided for estimating various lengths of body segments. It was suggested that by observing the mobility utilized and vertical distance from the floor where work was performed, the necessary physical agilities required could be identified. Relationships between mobility and functions (D.P.T.) and mobility and strength requirements were discussed. The analyst who integrates these relationships into their observation Techniques will be the most successful in efficiently, concisely, and accurately analyzing positions in industrial settings.

Interviewing and observation are two-thirds of the job analysis methodology. Chapter 5 will guide the analyst through the specific procedures of identifying and verifying the essential functions per ADA. In Chapter 6, the last third of the methodology, report writing guidelines are explained.

CHAPTER 5

ADA
ESSENTIAL FUNCTION
IDENTIFICATION

A job analysis of positions is critical for the identification of the essential functions and to verify that the specific requirements are job related and a business necessity.

ADA ESSENTIAL FUNCTION IDENTIFICATION

Now that you have analyzed the position, how do you determine what functions are essential and what functions are marginal?

As discussed in Chapter 2, Human Resource Managers utilize job related data for numerous purposes. The development of selection criteria and directing placement are two examples. A job analysis of positions is critical for the identification of the essential functions and to verify that the specified requirements are job related and a business necessity. A job analysis should be performed to gather job related data before determining specific functions are either essential or marginal.

PURPOSE

Prior to evaluating either existing job descriptions or conducting job analyses to identify the fundamental duties and qualifications, the Analyst must very clearly understand:

The **purpose** or reason for the position to exist in the organization.

The identification of the purpose or the reason for the position to exist in the organization is fundamental for determining essential versus marginal functions. Do the fundamental duties required of an individual support the purpose of the position or support the reason that the position exists in the organization? The fundamental or essential duties of a position should support the purpose, intent, and reason for which the position exists in the organization. (Refer to Chapter 3, Conducting the On–Site Interview, Step 3).

PRIMARY CONSIDERATIONS

There are two primary considerations for verifying if a function is essential. The first primary consideration is determining whether the incumbents actually perform the function.

1. **Do current employees in the position actually perform the function in question?**

If the function is not performed or the performance of the function is not essential to carrying out the overall purpose of the position, then the function may not be essential but may in fact be marginal.

The second primary consideration is:

2. **Would removing the function fundamentally change the position?**

Two specific questions to ask are:

A) Would removing the function interrupt the flow or the output of the required work?

B) Would the purpose or the reason for the position to exist be severely depleted if the function was removed?

If the conclusion to either of these two primary considerations is "No", then the function should be considered marginal. If both of the primary considerations are "Yes", then the function is likely to be essential. For further verification, analyze the function referring the three secondary considerations.

SECONDARY CONSIDERATIONS

There are three secondary considerations when analyzing whether a function is essential or marginal:

1. Does the position exist to perform the function?

The analyst must determine how the function directly supports the reason that the position exists.

For Example, a person is hired to visually inspect the doors and windows of a building to ensure they are locked during non-business hours. The mobility and vision abilities required to inspect are essential, because this is the reason the position exists.

2. Are there a limited number of employees who can perform the function?

A consideration of the size of the work force and the fluctuating demands of the business may determine if a particular function has to be performed by a specific individual due to the lack of other individuals available to distribute the work.

For Example, in a large work force there may be more opportunity to distribute functions among workers versus in a small work force where fewer people are available to perform more diverse functions.

3. Is the function highly specialized?

Is the worker hired for the specialization? Is the specialization required to carry out the purpose of the position? The frequency in which the specialization is required is not as critical as the need for the specialization to carry out the overall purpose of the position.

For example, a company is expanding their engineering department due to business growth. An engineering supervisor is being hired in the department. The department uses computer aided drafting (CAD) software called "Expert CAD" for its engineering drawings. It is essential the engineering supervisor be computer and "Expert CAD" software experienced.

In analyzing the individual functions of a position the above five considerations are paramount in determining if a function is essential or marginal.

EVIDENCE

The employer may also gather and document evidence to support their belief that particular functions are essential. Examples of evidence include:

1. **The employer's judgment as to which functions are essential.** (An employer does not have to lower quality, quantity or standards of work, but the job specifications have to be a business necessity.)

2. **A written job description prepared before advertising or interviewing applicants for a position.** (A current job description identifies the purpose of the position and includes the functions necessary to perform the position.)

3. **The amount of time spent performing each function.** (Time alone is not the most relevant indicator of what functions are essential.)

4. **The consequences of not requiring the employee to perform the function.** (Serious consequences may identify a function as being essential.)

5. **The terms of a collective bargaining agreement.** (Collective bargaining agreements are only a possible form of evidence and not conclusive evidence of what is essential.)

6. **The work experience of past and current incumbents in the position.** (Functions actually being performed provide significant evidence as to their being essential.)

7. **The employer's organizational structure and nature of work operations may determine if a function is essential.** (The employer will not be told how to run their business, but organizational structures and operations cannot purposefully discriminate against individuals with disabilities seeking employment.)

ESSENTIAL FUNCTION CRITERIA CHECKLIST

The Essential Function Criteria Checklist was developed to provide a systematic approach to evaluating functions and to document what evidence is available to support the employer's judgment that a function is essential. The checklist should be completed for each duty or function presented for consideration.

The two primary questions to ask when determining if a function is essential are:

1. Does the incumbent actually perform the function?

2. Would removing the function fundamentally change the outcome or purpose of the position?

Both of these questions need to be answered **"yes"** if the function is to be considered essential. If either of these two questions are marked **"No"**, then the following three questions should be considered to determine if the function is essential:

1. Does the position exist to perform the function?

2. Are there limited number of employees who can perform the function?

3. Is the function highly specialized?

If **"Yes"** was answered to the primary questions 1 and 2 and **"Yes"** to the first question, and **"Yes"** or **"No"** to the second and third questions, then the duty or function would be considered essential.

Example:

ESSENTIAL FUNCTIONS CRITERIA CHECKLIST

POSITION TITLE: _WAREHOUSE WORKER_

FUNCTION: _UNLOADS MERCHANDISE FROM INCOMING CONVEYANCES USING HANDCARTS, ETC._

(Complete a checklist for each function)

PRIMARY CONSIDERATIONS	YES	NO
1. Do incumbents actually perform the function?	☒	❏
2. Would removing the function fundamentally change the position?	☒	❏

REASONS TO CONSIDER	YES	NO
1. Does the position exist to perform the function?	☒	❏
2. Are there a limited number of employees who could perform the function?	☒	❏
3. Are the functions highly specialized?	❏	☒

EVIDENCE TO CONSIDER	YES	NO
1. Employers judgement that the function is essential?	☒	❏
2. Does a written Job Description include the function?	☒	❏
3. Is there a significant amount of time spent performing the function?	☒	❏
4. Are there serious consequences in not performing the function?	❏	☒
5. Is there a Collective Bargaining Agreement?	❏	☒

Function is Essential:	☒	❏

Analyst Name _____ Date _____

Incumbent's Name _____ Date _____

Supervisor Name _____ Date _____

JOB SPECIFICATIONS

After the **fundamental duties** are identified, verified and determined to be essential or marginal, then the **job specifications** must be identified, verified and evaluated to determine whether they are essential.

The job specifications are comprised of qualifications and requirements. They would include the educational, language, math and reasoning abilities required, physical and mental demands required, environmental conditions, perceptual and visual abilities required and certifications and licenses required for employment. These specifications, and how to identify them at the job site, are discussed in Chapter 3 and 4 .

To determine if the specifications are required to perform the function, ask:

1. If the qualification was eliminated, would the individual be able to perform the function?

2. Would altering the requirements alter the manner and means but not necessarily alter the ability to carry out the essential function?

3. Is an accommodation required to allow the individual to perform the function?

The evidence in which the employer can accumulate to support their opinion of which specifications are essential include:

1. Written job descriptions with job specifications identified.

2. Identification of the amount of time spent using or performing the specification.

3. Identification of the consequences if the specifications were not used.

4. Verification that workers have actually been performing the functions using the specifications.

5. Production standards and workload documents.

6. Collective Bargaining Agreements.

7. The employer's judgment.

The checklist or worksheet of the data and evidence collected when conducting a job analysis would be impactful. It can be used to support the employers position of non-discrimination against an individual who thought he/she was qualified for a particular position.

CHAPTER 6

REPORT WRITING GUIDELINES

Guidelines for writing the individual Function
Sentence and the Job description Report.

REPORT WRITING GUIDELINES

HOW TO WRITE A FUNCTION (DUTY/TASK) SENTENCE

Once the Analyst has obtained the position information it is necessary to write the function sentence. The most accepted model for describing a worker situation has been developed by the U. S. Department of Labor. This model permits the most complex duties to be stated in brief but declarative sentences. Each sentence will state:

1. What the worker does by using a specific **action verb** which introduces the duty or task sentence;

2. To whom or to what the worker performs it, by stating the **object** of the verb;

3. What is produced by the expected **outcome** of the verb;

4. What **machines, equipment, tools** or **work aids** are used to produce the outcome.

The subject (the worker, occupational group or job class title) of the duty sentence is implied, not specifically expressed in the written sentence. In other words, personal pronouns or repeating the occupational group or job class title is not necessary when writing the duty/task sentences.

The action verb is synonymous with the function which is being described. Two questions which are generally asked are:

1. How specific does the action verb have to be?

2. Should duty/task sentences be narrow or broad in terms of worker activities?

The action verb needs to be specific enough to inform the reader of the worker function. Action verbs that have several meanings should be avoided so as not to confuse the reader. Your practice with writing duty/task sentences will enhance your ability to select the proper action verbs.

Poor action verbs commonly found in job descriptions are:

- Assumes
- Participates
- Supports
- Handles
- Assists
- Responsible for

These are poor verbs due to the variety of connotations and meanings. A partial list of commonly used action verbs are listed in Appendix E.

A question commonly asked is, "What duties or tasks of a worker's position should be described in a duty sentence?" The Analyst should concentrate on writing only the critical and significant duties/tasks of a position. Usually this is 4 to 12 different duties/tasks per position. The exact number will of course vary with different positions. However, the overall aim should be to cover all the critical and significant activities in which the worker is involved with as few sentences as possible. All things considered, a broad approach would be the most practical, providing the best structure for further analysis and use of the gathered information.

The framework for the duty/task sentence structure is constant:

An implied subject, an action verb, object, expected outcome, and Machines, Equipment, Tools and Work Aids (M,E,T,WA).

The **implied subject** which is the worker, occupational group or job class title is not written throughout the entire job description. The **action verbs** represent the activities of the position. The **object** is either data, people or a thing. In the case of a data function, the object is information. In the case of a people function, the object is usually to whom a service is being rendered. In a thing function, the object is usually a machine, equipment, tool, work aid, materials, substances or products. The **outcome or results** statement represents why the object is acting.

EXAMPLE OF DUTY/TASK SENTENCES:

ACTION VERB	IMMEDIATE OBJECT	OUTCOME OF ACTION	M,E,T,WA
TURNS	screws and nuts (thing)	to adjust motion of machine,	using wrenches, screwdrivers and pliers.
READS	blueprint or job order (data)	to determine dimensions and tolerances of workpiece.	
COUNTS	stock, material, or merchandise on hand (thing)	to inventory records.	
TESTS	customer's hearing (people)	to determine need for hearing aid,	using audiometer.

Per the *"Revised Handbook for Analyzing Jobs"*, the following style conventions are recommended for preparing duty/task sentences:

1. A terse, direct style should be used.

2. The present tense, third person singular should be used throughout.

3. Each sentence should begin with an action verb.

4. Each sentence must reflect a specifically stated objective or an objective implied in such manner as to be obvious to the reader. A single verb may sometimes reflect both objective and worker action.

5. All words should impart necessary information; others shouldbe omitted. Every precaution should be taken to use words that have only one possible connotation and that specifically describes the manner in which the work is accomplished.

6. The description of tasks should reflect the assigned work.

7. Avoid excessive, technical language. The Analyst's job is to make a technical subject understandable to persons unfamiliar with the subject. Where technical words are universally used throughout the industry, they become usable occupational data.

8. Avoid being pompous. Use a one-syllable word rather than a four-syllable word if both convey the same meaning.

   "A superfluity of culinary assistance is apt to exercise a detrimental effect upon the consomme." A sentence such as "Too many cooks spoil the broth" is sufficient.

9. Avoid the use of slang and colloquialisms. The meanings of such terms are usually obscure. If they are universally understood throughout the industry, however, they may be included in the description of tasks with an explanatory phrase.

10. The use of poetic license is a barrier to precise communication and should be avoided.

    "This stroke requires great incubus of judgment in elevation and strength and betrays the hand of the master when successful." An incubus is a form of demon and no person was betrayed.

11. The word used must reflect exactly what is intended.

    "The engineer wrote a partial account..." (incomplete or prejudiced?)

    "Although the proportions of all males and females in ages 16-45 are essentially the same..." does the Analyst mean percentage?

    "...cattle usually and commonly embraced in dairying..."

12. Select the word that best reflects the thought.

    Judgment is held in suspense; a chemical is held in suspension.

    A problem is unsolvable; an ore is insoluble.

    Steam was discovered; the radio was invented.

13. Do not compress more than one or two thoughts into a single sentence. Such compression is usually accomplished at the expense of clarity and readability.

    "Mixes, blends, purifies, screens, and extrudes smokeless and plastic propellant powders, cast propellant charges, and high explosive powders on a small lot basis, including manual and machine operations for nickel mercury amalgam."

    "Trims flash from rubber gaskets, rings, swim fins and goggles, handlebar grips, and other molded rubber products, using scissors, knives, and cutting die and mallet, by holding product against revolving abrasive wheel or trimming knives, or by means of a tumbling barrel in which flash is made brittle with dry ice."

14. Make active and positive statements rather than passive, negative, or conditional ones.

    "An outline...may be of help to..." (Delete underlined words)

    "The ore is not uncommon in..." (The ore is common in...)

    "Makes analysis of..." (Analyzes...)

15. Avoid superlatives and certain types of adverbs. Superlatives give a false emphasis and certain adverbs weaken the verb they modify.

    Avoid *"most"*, *"best"*, and similar superlatives.

    "Very straight" doesn't make the object any straighter.

    "Perfectly perpendicular" fits the same category.

16. Do not use the definite or indefinite articles, "the", "a", or "an". Clarity and readability are not lost when they are not used.

    "Inserts tubes into designated sockets of tube tester and observes meter readings..."

17. Never use "etc." or "and so forth." If there are no additional examples to be included, end the sentence at the last example. However, to denote an incomplete list, the Analyst can use the expression "such as."

    "Examines watch dials for defects, such as scratches, finger marks, dirt, and uncentered cannon and fourth wheel pinions, using loupe."

18. Avoid using attributes.

    "Complex controls, intimate knowledge, large billet, heavy tool, small spring..."

    The precise meanings of such attributes are a matter of individual interpretation. One cannot expect the reader to interpret them in the same manner as the writer. The job description itself must convey the desired impression.

"Transfers watch parts from...to holding fixture, using tweezers and magnifying lens."

The impression left here is that the watch parts must be "minute".

19. Pretend that such words as "necessary, proper, and appropriate" do not exist.

    "Selects proper cutting tool to..."

    The reader cannot be expected to understand what is "proper" or the extent of judgment that enters into the selection process. These must be explained; as soon as the explanation is made, there is no longer any need for the word "proper."

    "Selects cutting tool depending on depth and diameter of hole to be drilled..."

20. Linking certain prepositions with certain verbs sometimes results in a looseness of language. Yet certain prepositions idiomatically follow certain words.

account for	aware of	adhere to	differ from (quality)
Differ with (opinion)	Parallel with	preference for	Perpendicular to

21. Word sequence can be important.

    "These ladles only were filled with molten steel."

    "These ladles were filled only with molten steel."

22. The word "may" is not considered synonymous with "occasionally" and should never be used. If a work element is performed occasionally or infrequently, it may be written as a regular work element which begins with the words "occasionally" or "periodically."

23. The job description should not contain the phrase "Performs any combination of the following duties".

24. Always use a comma before "utilizing" and "using" in sentence.

25. A comma is usually used before phrases beginning with "such as".

26. The Analyst should keep in mind the necessity of stating a duty/task completely but should not allow the explanation to develop into a motion study. For example, it may be stated that an inspector of small parts *"Slides fingertips over machine edges to detect ragged edges and burrs."*

On the other hand, it would be absurd to state: *"Raises right hand one foot to table height, superimposes hand over mechanical part and, by depressing the first and second fingers to the machine part and moving arm slowly sideways about six inches, feels with fingertips for snags or pricks that are indicative of surface irregularities".*

JOB DESCRIPTION REPORT

A job description is a document listing the specific duties, qualifications and requirements necessary to achieve the intended results or outcome of a position. Per the ADA, a job description document may be used as a source of evidence to support the nondiscrimination of an otherwise qualified individual with a disability. It is also helpful in establishing appropriate qualification standards, preparing for and conducting applicant interviews, preparing recruiting announcements and in the selection of qualified people. It will also help to identify what accommodations may be necessary for a qualified individual with disability to perform in a position.

A job description document intended to be used as evidence of essential functions should be:

A) developed following completion of an objective job analysis,

B) prepared to represent the essential duties, qualifications and requirements of a position,

C) current,

D) specific and not include ambiguous references to duties unless they are accepted as marginal duties.

A job description document is a summary of the important facts about a particular position. It states in a concise, clear way, the information obtained from the job analysis concerning:

1. The job title—A descriptive title for the position.

2. Purpose of position—A brief summary stating the overall goal of the position in the organization.

3. The essential functions—The major responsibilities or fundamental duties of the position.

4. Marginal functions—The non-essential duties of the position.

5. Relationships—To whom and by whom the position is supervised, reports to or works with.

6. Position information—The job code, salary grade, department and work unit name, union affiliation and related information specifying the role of the position in the organization.

7. Job specifications—The qualifications and requirements necessary to perform adequately in the position.

The job specifications describe those requirements that would be expected of anyone who is placed in the position. It also identifies any unusual, hazardous, or environmental conditions which the job holder must be prepared to accept. Job specifications describe the desired attributes of an employee for successful performance in the position. The job specifications state in a concise, clear way:

1. Education—That education that is really necessary for the position such as, high school graduate, college education, trade school or other special training.

2. Experience—the amount of previous and related experience which a new employee would be expected to have.

3. Knowledge/Skills—The specific knowledge and skills which the position requires for successful performance.

4. Licenses/Certifications—The specific certifications or licenses required to perform in the position.

5. Physical and Mental Requirements—The maximum abilities required for performance in the position. Related specifically to essential functions and the outcome or expected results of the position not necessarily the customary manner or means in which it is performed.

6. Environment—The specific environmental conditions in which the individual must be adaptable to working in to be successful in the position.

7. Machines, Equipment, Tools and Work Aids—The special experience or skill requirements to operate machines, equipment, tools and work aids as related to performance in the position.

SUMMARY

For your review and practice a complete Job Analysis Worksheet and a complete Job Description Form for the **warehouse worker** are provided at the end of this chapter. Additionally "Job Descriptions" (pre-ADA) are in Appendix A, completed Job Analysis Worksheets are in Appendix B and completed Job Descriptions are in Appendix C.

As an excercise review these documents as examples of the data gathering and documenting techniques presented in Chapters 3, 4 and 5. Note the benefits of the Job Analysis Worksheet and Job Description format.

When reviewing these documents, keep in mind the techniques previously discussed including:

• Selection of the essential functions, requirements and qualifications.

• Identification of the purpose of a position, job class, and/or occupational groups.

• Listing the Machines, Equipment, Tools and Work Aids.

Employer Prepared Job Description (Pre–ADA)

DATE	GRADE	JOB CODE
22 June 89	4	738-01

JOB TITLE: Warehouse Worker (Semiskilled)

JOB LOCATION: ABC Distribution Center

PAY PLAN: Trades

GENERAL FUNCTION

Under designated supervision, performs a variety of repetitive warehousing duties primarily physical in nature in the receiving, storage, sorting, and/or shipping functions. A supervisor or higher grade warehouse worker gives specific instructions on how to do any new operations, and reviews work to see that it meets requirements.

DUTIES AND RESPONSIBILITIES:

1. Unloads merchandise from incoming conveyances. Compares markings and quantities of incoming items with those shown on receiving reports. Makes appropriate entries on receiving documents except for signing freight bills and receiving reports. Marks freight register numbers on cases and receiving documents, and attaches location labels on merchandise.

2. Operates a ticket printing machine to print prices, merchandise identification, and associated information on tickets to be attached to merchandise as required or directed.

3. May move merchandise from location to location by hand, pallet jack, hand truck, carts, or similar manual equipment if necessary due to conveyor system malfunction.

4. May sort/select merchandise from storage, and arrange them on conveyor systems in the order set by light and bell signals or other clearly established procedures. Verifies type and quantity of merchandise on branch requisition or other

   shipping documents.

5. Participates in the taking of periodic and special inventories.

6. Complies with established safety, security, and fire prevention procedures and directives.

7. Performs other related duties as assigned.

Supervisory Controls: Works under immediately available supervision. Receives assignments orally or in writing which indicates where and how clearly identified items are to be received, stored, maintained or assembled for issue and shipment. Completes repeated assignments independently in accordance with original instructions. Supervisor or higher grade worker checks work in progress and upon completion to see that requirements are met.

Working Conditions: Works inside and outside. May work in areas that are hot, cold, damp, drafty, or poorly lighted. Work may be dirty, dusty, and greasy. Frequently exposed to the possibility of cuts, scrapes, and bruises, falls from ladders, or injury from mechanical conveyor systems or other material handling equipment.

Physical Effort: Works on hard surfaces in areas that require standing, stooping, bending and working in tiring and uncomfortable positions. May be required to work at a rapid pace for long periods of time. Frequently lifts and carries objects weighing up to 30 pounds, and occasionally 30 to 70 pounds.

Qualification Requirements—Education/Experience/Abilities/Skills

Completion of high school or the equivalent. Creditable job-related experience may be substituted for the education requirement on a nine-months-for-nine-months basis. Six months of progressively responsible general work experience which may have involved maintaining records, receiving, screening, reviewing, and verifying documents, and preparing and/or verifying the validity of documents with which the organization is concerned. Graduation from high school, or equivalent education may be substituted for required experience.

Analyst Completed Job Description (Post ADA)

JOB DESCRIPTION

Position Title: _WAREHOUSE WORKER_

Job Code/Labor Grade: _738-01/4_

Department/Division: _RECEIVING_

Work Unit: _DOCK_   NO. of EE's: _4_

Shift Assignment: A _____   B ___X___   C _____

Union Affiliation: _NONE_

Supervisor: _JACK BARLEY_   Phone Number: _000-0000_

Job Analyst: _R. THRUSH_   Phone Number: _000-0000_

ESSENTIAL FUNCTIONS STATEMENT

Purpose: _RECEIVE, MARK, STORE AND SORT MERCHANDISE PER ESTABLISHED PROCEDURES._

Functions: _1. UNLOADS MERCHANDISE FROM INCOMING CONVEYANCES USING HAND CART, ETC._

2. VISUALLY VERIFIES TYPE AND QUANTITY OF MERCHANDISE WITH RECEIVING AND SHIPPING DOCUMENTATION.

3. MARKS IDENTIFICATION DETAILS ONTO MERCHANDISE AND DOCUMENTATION USING WRITING UTENSILS AND TICKET PRINTING MACHINE.

4. SELECTS AND ARRANGES STORED MERCHANDISE ONTO CONVEYOR PER ESTABLISHED PROCEDURES.

Write additional functions on a separate piece of paper and attach to form.

JOB QUALIFICATIONS

Education: _HIGH SCHOOL GRADUATE_

Experience: _6 MONTHS RELATED GENERAL WORK EXPERIENCE_

Skills/Knowledge/Abilities: _MAINTAIN, SCREEN, RECORD, REVIEW, VERIFY AND PREPARE DOCUMENTS._

Licenses/Certificates: _NONE_

Machine, Equipment, Tool Skills: _TO UTILIZE MATERIAL MOVING AIDS SUCH AS PALLET JACK, TWO WHEEL DOLLY, CARTS AND CONVEYOR SYSTEM._

JOB REQUIREMENTS

PHYSICAL REQUIREMENTS

	NUMBER OF HOURS							NUMBER OF HOURS				
	0	0-3	3-5	5-8	8+			0	0-3	3-5	5-8	8+
1. SITTING	X	❑	❑	❑	❑	15.	REPETITIVE USE–HAND					
2. STANDING	❑	❑	X	❑	❑		A. DOMINANT	❑	❑	❑	X	❑
3. WALKING	❑	❑	X	❑	❑		B. NON-DOMINANT	❑	❑	X	❑	❑
4. REACHING OVERHEAD	❑	❑	X	❑	❑		C. BOTH	❑	❑	❑	❑	❑
5. BENDING OVER	❑	❑	X	❑	❑	16.	GRASPING-LIGHT					
6. CROUCHING	❑	X	❑	❑	❑		A. DOMINANT	❑	❑	X	❑	❑
7. KNEELING	❑	X	❑	❑	❑		B. NON-DOMINANT	❑	❑	X	❑	❑
8. CRAWLING	X	❑	❑	❑	❑		C. BOTH	❑	❑	❑	❑	❑
9. CLIMBING	❑	X	❑	❑	❑		GRASPING-FIRM/STRONG					
10. BALANCING	❑	X	❑	❑	❑		D. DOMINANT	❑	❑	X	❑	❑
11. PUSHING/PULLING	❑	❑	X	❑	❑		E. NON-DOMINANT	❑	X	❑	❑	❑
12. LIFTING/CARRYING							F. BOTH	❑	❑	❑	❑	❑
A. 10 LBS OR LESS	❑	❑	X	❑	❑	17.	FINGER DEXTERITY					
B. 11-25 LBS	❑	❑	X	❑	❑		A. DOMINANT	❑	❑	❑	❑	❑
C. 25-50 LBS	❑	❑	X	❑	❑		B. NON-DOMINANT	❑	❑	❑	❑	❑
D. 51-75 LBS	❑	X	❑	❑	❑		C. BOTH	❑	❑	X	❑	❑
E. 76-100 LBS	X	❑	❑	❑	❑	18.	VISION					
F. OVER 100 LBS	X	❑	❑	❑	❑		A. ACUITY, FAR	❑	❑	❑	X	❑
13. DRIVING	X	❑	❑	❑	❑		B. ACUITY, NEAR	❑	❑	❑	X	❑
14. REPETITIVE USE-FOOT							C. DEPTH PERCEPTION	X	❑	❑	❑	❑
A. RIGHT ONLY	X	❑	❑	❑	❑		D. FIELD OF VISION	X	❑	❑	❑	❑
B. LEFT ONLY	X	❑	❑	❑	❑		E. ACCOMMODATION	X	❑	❑	❑	❑
C. BOTH	X	❑	❑	❑	❑		F. COLOR VISION	❑	X	❑	❑	❑

ADA–Essential Function Identification

Mental Requirements

☒ Reading, Simple	☐ Spatial	☒ Tending
☐ Reading, Complex	☒ Form	☐ Precision Working
☒ Writing, Simple	☒ Clerical	☒ Follow Instructions
☐ Writing, Complex	☐ Compiling	☐ Influence Others
☒ Math Skills, Simple	☐ Coordination	☒ Time Requirement
☐ Math Skills, Complex	☐ Analyzing	☒ Memorization
☒ Tasks, Simple	☐ Synthesizing	☐ Problem Solving
☐ Tasks, Complex	☐ Supervising	☐ Independent Judgement
	☐ Instructing	☐ Decision Making
	☐ Driving	

Work Environment

☐ Works Alone	☐ Confined Areas	☐ Electrical Devices
☒ Works with Others	☐ Extreme Heat	☒ Mechanical Devices
☒ Works Around Others	☐ Extreme Cold	☐ Computer Equipment
☒ Verbal Contact w/Others	☒ Wet and/or Humid	☐ Pneumatic Devices
☒ Face-to-Face Contact	☐ Noise	☐ Flame/Heat Generated
☒ Shift Work	☐ Vibration	Devices
☐ Extended Day	☐ Solvents/Oils	☒ Moving Objects
☒ Inside	☒ Fumes/Odors	☐ High Places
☐ Outside	☒ Dirt/Dust	☒ Slippery Surfaces
	☐ Gases	
	☐ Explosives	

Analyst Name _____   Date _____

Supervisors Name_____   Date _____

Approval Date _____

ANALYST COMPLETED JOB ANALYSIS WORKSHEET

ESSENTIAL FUNCTIONS–DEMANDS JOB ANALYSIS WORKSHEET

Date *3-16-93*   Job Analyst *R. THRUSH*

JOB INFORMATION

Title *WAREHOUSE WORKER*   Employer *ABC DISTRIBUTION CENTER*

Job Code *738-01*   Labor Grade *4*   Salary/Rate *6.95 PER HR.*

Department *RECEIVING*   Shift Assignment: A _____   B *X*   C _____

Work Unit *DOCK*   Number Of Employees *4*

Union Affiliation *NONE*

Supervisor(s) _____   Phone No(s). _____

            JACK BARLEY   *000-0000*

            _____   _____

Incumbent(s) _____   Badge/SSN _____

            HENRY CAPPS   *00349*

            _____   _____

Job Description: Reviewed _____*X*_____   To Update _____   Not-Available _____

JOB SUMMARY

Reason the position exists (purpose):

The purpose of this position is to *RECEIVE, MARK, STORE AND SORT*
MERCHANDISE PER ESTABLISHED PROCEDURES.

_____

_____

_____

_____

Production or Workload

MAINTAIN A PACE APPROPRIATE FOR THE DAILY WORKLOAD

_____

_____

_____

ADA–Essential Function Identification

JOB FUNCTIONS

Essential Functions: Identify the critical duties actually performed by incumbents to fulfill the purpose of this position.

Write in prescribed sentence structure: action verb, object, [to] outcome, using M, E, T, W/A (machines, equipment, etc.).

Mark the "critical" box if not performing the duty would interrupt the flow of work. Include the daily % of time spent performing the critical duties. May not equal 100% due to performance of marginal duties.

Daily % Time	Critical	Action Verb	Object	[To] Outcome/METW/A
10%	✔	Reads	Instructions	To complete the form
40%	✔	UNLOADS	MERCHANDISE	FROM INCOMING CONVEYANCES USING HANDCART, ETC.
20%	✔	VISUALLY VERIFIES	TYPE AND QUANTITY OF MERCHANDISE	WITH RECEIVING AND SHIPPING DOCUMENTATION
20%	✔	MARKS	IDENTIFICATION DETAILS	ONTO MERCHANDISE AND DOCUMENTATION USING WRITING UTENSILS AND TICKETS
20%	✔	SELECTS AND ARRANGES	STORED MERCHANDISE	ONTO CONVEYOR PER ESTABLISHED PROCEDURES

ESSENTIAL FUNCTIONS CRITERIA CHECKLIST

POSITION TITLE: _WAREHOUSE WORKER_

FUNCTION: _UNLOADS MERCHANDISE FROM INCOMING CONVEYANCES USING HANDCARTS, ETC._

(Complete a checklist for each function)

PRIMARY CONSIDERATIONS	YES	No
1. Do incumbents actually perform the function?	☒	❏
2. Would removing the function fundamentally change the position?	☒	❏

REASONS TO CONSIDER	YES	No
1. Does the position exist to perform the function?	☒	❏
2. Are there a limited number of employees who could perform the function?	☒	❏
3. Are the functions highly specialized?	❏	☒

EVIDENCE TO CONSIDER	YES	No
1. Employers judgement that the function is essential?	☒	❏
2. Does a written Job Description include the function?	☒	❏
3. Is there a significant amount of time spent performing the function?	☒	❏
4. Are there serious consequences in not performing the function?	❏	☒
5. Is there a Collective Bargaining Agreement?	❏	☒

Function is Essential: ☒ ❏

Analyst Name _____ Date _____

Incumbent's Name _____ Date _____

Supervisor Name _____ Date _____

ORGANIZATIONAL RELATIONSHIPS

Identify as specifically as possible the relationship of the assigned work unit to the department and to the organization as a whole. Briefly state the overall purpose of the work unit and/or department to the organization. Sketch an organizational flowchart of the relationship of the work unit and/or department to the nearest related work units or departments.

Identify as specifically as possible the specific names and titles of the people who report to this position, and the name and title who this position reports to.

```
                    ┌─────────────────────────┐
                    │   SHIPPING/RECEIVING     │
                    │      WAREHOUSE           │
                    └─────────────────────────┘
                                │
                          ┌──────────────────────┐
                          │  MATERIAL DISPATCHER  │
                          └──────────────────────┘
                                │
        ┌───────────────────────┼───────────────────────┐
  ┌─────────────┐        ┌─────────────┐        ┌──────────────────┐
  │  SHIPPING   │        │  RECEIVING  │        │ FLEET MAINTENANCE │
  │ SUPERVISOR  │        │ SUPERVISOR  │        │   SUPERVISOR      │
  └─────────────┘        └─────────────┘        └──────────────────┘
                                │
        ┌───────────────────────┼───────────────────────┐
  ┌─────────────┐        ┌─────────────┐        ┌──────────────────┐
  │    DOCK     │        │  STOCKING   │        │    MANIFEST      │
  │    CREW     │        │    CREW     │        │ PREPARATION UNIT │
  └─────────────┘        └─────────────┘        └──────────────────┘
        │
  ┌─────────────┐
  │  INCUMBENT  │
  └─────────────┘
```

JOB REQUIREMENTS

PHYSICAL FACTORS

KEY:	NP = Not Present	O = 1/3 of the day
	F = 1/3–2/3 of the day	C = Over 2/3 of the day

FACTOR 1: STRENGTH

MOBILITY **FREQUENCY**

		NP	O	F	C
A.	Stand __45__ % of time __3.5__ hrs/day	☐	☐	☒	☐
B.	Walk __55__ % of time __4.5__ hrs/day	☐	☐	☒	☐
C.	Sit __0__ % of time __0__ hrs/day	☒	☐	☐	☐
	__100%__ __4/⑧/10__ hrs/day				

COMMENTS: _WALKS UPON CONCRETE LEVEL SURFACE IN WAREHOUSE, STANDS ON RUBBER MAT AT CONVEYOR AND MACHINES._

LIFTING **FREQUENCY**

	NP	O	F	C
up to 5 lbs	☐	☐	☒	☐
6 - 10 lbs	☐	☐	☒	☐
11 - 20 lbs	☐	☐	☒	☐
21 - 25 lbs	☐	☐	☒	☐
26 - 50 lbs	☐	☒	☐	☐
51 - 75 lbs	☐	☒	☐	☐
76 - 100 lbs	☒	☐	☐	☐
Over 100 lbs	☒	☐	☐	☐

COMMENTS: (Heaviest item and range of vertical distance) _SURFACE FREIGHT CARTONS MAY WEIGH A MAXIMUM OF 70 POUNDS. MOST CARTONS HANDLED WEIGH LESS THAN 30 POUNDS. THE CARTONS ARE LIFTED A MAXIMUM OF 35" ONTO OR OFF OF CONVEYOR FROM/TO WAREHOUSE PALLET ON FLOOR._

FACTOR 1:   STRENGTH   Continued

CARRYING   FREQUENCY

	NP	O	F	C
up to 5 lbs	☐	☐	☐	☒
6 - 10 lbs	☐	☐	☐	☒
11 - 20 lbs	☐	☐	☒	☐
21 - 25 lbs	☐	☒	☐	☐
26 - 50 lbs	☒	☐	☐	☐
51 - 75 lbs	☒	☐	☐	☐
76 - 100 lbs	☒	☐	☐	☐
Over 100 lbs	☒	☐	☐	☐

COMMENTS: (Heaviest item and range of horizontal distance) _INFREQUENTLY A CARTON WEIGHING UP TO 50 POUNDS IS CARRIED 40', THE LENGTH OF A SHIPPING CONTAINER. MOST CARTONS ARE CARRIED LESS THAN 15 FEET AND WEIGH LESS THAN 30 POUNDS._

PUSHING/PULLING   FREQUENCY

	NP	O	F	C
5 lbs	☐	☐	☒	☐
6 - 10 lbs	☐	☐	☒	☐
11 - 20 lbs	☐	☐	☒	☐
21 - 25 lbs	☒	☐	☐	☐
26 - 50 lbs	☒	☐	☐	☐
51 - 75 lbs	☒	☐	☐	☐
76 - 100 lbs	☒	☐	☐	☐.
Over 100 lbs	☒	☐	☐	☐

COMMENTS: (Wheeled objects, Footpedal, Lever, Equipment or Hand tool) _USES PUSH/PULL MOTION TO MANUALLY MOVE CARTONS ON ROLLERS OF CONVEYORS SYSTEM._

FACTOR 2:   AGILITY

			NP	O	F	C
A.	Climbing		☐	☒	☐	☐
B.	Balancing		☒	☐	☐	☐
C.	Bending		☐	☐	☒	☐
D.	Stooping		☐	☒	☐	☐
E.	Crouching		☐	☒	☐	☐
F.	Kneeling		☐	☒	☐	☐

FACTOR 2:   AGILITY   Continued

FREQUENCY

		NP	O	F	C
G.	Crawling	☒	☐	☐	☐
H.	Running	☒	☐	☐	☐
I.	Twisting	☐	☒	☐	☐
J.	Turning	☐	☒	☐	☐
K.	Jumping	☒	☐	☐	☐

COMMENTS: _____

_____

_____

FACTOR 3:   DEXTERITY

FREQUENCY

		NP	O	F	C
A.	Grasping–Firm/Strong	☐	☐	☒	☐
B.	Finger Dexterity	☐	☐	☒	☐
C.	Reaching Forward	☐	☐	☒	☐
D.	Reaching Overhead	☐	☒	☐	☐
E.	Pinching	☐	☒	☐	☐
F.	Grasping–Light	☐	☒	☐	☐

Dominant hand: ☒ Right   ☐ Left   ☐ Both

COMMENTS: _____

_____

_____

FACTOR 4:   COORDINATION

FREQUENCY

		NP	O	F	C
A.	Eye - hand	☐	☐	☐	☒
B.	Eye - Hand - Foot	☒	☐	☐	☐
C.	Driving	☒	☐	☐	☐

COMMENTS: _____

_____

_____

FACTOR 5: VISION

FREQUENCY

		NP	O	F	C
A.	Acuity, Near	☐	☐	☐	☒
B.	Acuity, Far	☐	☐	☐	☒
C.	Depth Perception	☒	☐	☐	☐
D.	Accommodation	☒	☐	☐	☐
E.	Color Vision	☐	☒	☐	☐
F.	Field of Vision	☒	☐	☐	☐

COMMENTS: _____
_____
_____

FACTOR 6: TALKING

FREQUENCY

		NP	O	F	C
A.	Face-to-Face Contact	☐	☐	☒	☐
B.	Verbal Contact with Others	☐	☒	☐	☐
C.	Public	☐	☒	☐	☐

COMMENTS: _PRIMARILY CONVERSES WITH CO-WORKERS, TRUCK DRIVERS AND SUPERVISOR._
OCCASIONALLY ANSWERS THE TELEPHONE. OCCASIONALLY PROVIDES GENERAL
INFORMATION TO A CUSTOMER.

FACTOR 7: HEARING

FREQUENCY

		NP	O	F	C
A.	Normal Conversation	☐	☐	☐	☒
B.	Telephone Communication	☐	☒	☐	☐
C.	Earplugs Required	☒	☐	☐	☐

COMMENTS: _____
_____
_____

ENVIRONMENTAL FACTORS

		NP	O	F	C
A.	Works indoors	☐	☐	☐	☒
B.	Works outdoors	☒	☐	☐	☐
C.	Exposure to extreme hot or cold temperature	☒	☐	☐	☐
D.	Working at unprotected heights	☒	☐	☐	☐
E.	Being around moving machinery	☐	☐	☒	☐
F.	Exposure to marked changes in temperature/humidity	☐	☐	☒	☐
G.	Exposure to dust, fumes, smoke, gases, odors, mists or other irritating particles	☐	☐	☒	☐
	(specify) _____				
H.	Exposure to toxic or caustic chemicals	☒	☐	☐	☐
I.	Exposure to excessive noises	☒	☐	☐	☐
J.	Exposure to radiation or electrical energy	☒	☐	☐	☐
K.	Exposure to solvents, grease, or oils	☒	☐	☐	☐
L.	Exposure to slippery or uneven walking surfaces	☐	☒	☐	☐
M.	Working below ground	☒	☐	☐	☐
N.	Using computer (CRT) monitor	☒	☐	☐	☐
O.	Working with explosives	☒	☐	☐	☐
P.	Exposure to vibration	☒	☐	☐	☐
Q.	Exposure to flames or burning items	☒	☐	☐	☐
R.	Works around others	☐	☐	☐	☒
S.	Works alone	☒	☐	☐	☐
T.	Works with others	☐	☐	☒	☐

COMMENTS: (Describe special conditions) _____

_____

_____

SAFETY FACTORS

	PRESENT	NOT PRESENT
Material Safety Data Sheets (Verify Availability and Current)	☒	☐
Safety Equipment (Required to Wear)		
Safety Glasses	☐	☒
Ear Plugs	☐	☒
Hard Hat	☐	☒
Protective Clothing	☐	☒
Other _____	☐	☒
_____	☐	☐

MACHINES • EQUIPMENT • TOOLS • WORK AIDS

MACHINES

Devices which are a combination of mechanical parts, power actuated and designed to apply force to do work on or move materials or to process data. Vehicles are considered to be machines.

List	Skilled	OJT
NONE	❑	❑
	❑	❑
	❑	❑
	❑	❑
	❑	❑
	❑	❑
	❑	❑
	❑	❑
	❑	❑
	❑	❑

EQUIPMENT

Devices which are power actuated and generally designed to be portable and used to apply a force to do work on or move material or to process data.

List	Skilled	OJT
TICKET MACHINE	❑	☒
CONVEYOR ROLLERS, PERMANENT	☒	❑
	❑	❑
	❑	❑
	❑	❑
	❑	❑
	❑	❑
	❑	❑
	❑	❑
	❑	❑

MACHINES • EQUIPMENT • TOOLS • WORK AIDS

TOOLS

Devices or implements which are not power actuated and are manipulated by hand to do work on or move materials.

LIST	SKILLED	OJT
PALLET JACK	☒	☐
HAND TRUCK	☒	☐
CARTS	☒	☐
TAPER	☐	☒
	☐	☐
	☐	☐
	☐	☐
	☐	☐
	☐	☐
	☐	☐
	☐	☐

WORK AIDS

Items not considered to be a machine, equipment or tool yet are necessary for carrying out the work.

LIST	SKILLED	OJT
LADDER	☒	☐
WRITING UTENSILS	☒	☐
MARKING UTENSILS	☒	☐
STAPLER	☒	☐
	☐	☐
	☐	☐
	☐	☐
	☐	☐
	☐	☐
	☐	☐

KEY

OJT– The worker will need to learn to use upon commencing work in the position

SKILLED– The worker would need to have experience prior to commencing work in the position

JOB QUALIFICATIONS

MENTAL FACTORS

FACTOR 1   GENERAL EDUCATION DEVELOPMENT

REASONING   PRESENT   NOT PRESENT

	PRESENT	NOT PRESENT
Deal with abstract and concrete variables, define problems, collect data, establish facts, and draw valid conclusions	☐	☒
Interpret instructions furnished in written, oral, diagrammatic, or schedule form	☐	☒
Deal with problems from standard situations	☐	☒
Carry out detailed but uninvolved written or oral instructions	☒	☐
Carry out single one or two step instructions	☒	☐

MATHEMATICS   PRESENT   NOT PRESENT

COMPLEX SKILLS

	PRESENT	NOT PRESENT
Business math, algebra, geometry, shopmath or statistics	☐	☒

SIMPLE SKILLS

	PRESENT	NOT PRESENT
Add, subtract, multiply and divide whole numbers and fractions, make change, calculate time, calculate simple measurements	☒	☐

READING   PRESENT   NOT PRESENT

COMPLEX SKILLS

	PRESENT	NOT PRESENT
Comprehend newspapers, manuals, journals, instructions in use and maintenance of shop tools and equipment, safety rules and procedures and drawings	☐	☒

SIMPLE SKILLS

	PRESENT	NOT PRESENT
English at the 6th grade level (tested), comprehend simple instructions or notations from a log book	☒	☐

FACTOR 1	GENERAL EDUCATION DEVELOPMENT	continued

WRITING	PRESENT	NOT PRESENT

COMPLEX SKILLS

Prepare business letters, summaries of reports using prescribed format and conforming to all rules of spelling, punctuation, grammar, diction and style .... ☐   ☒

SIMPLE SKILLS

English sentences containing subject, verb and object; names and addresses, complete job application or notations in a log book .... ☒   ☐

FACTOR 2	EDUCATIONAL ACHIEVEMENT

High School: ☒ Yes ☐ No

College Degree: ☐ Associate   ☐ Bachelor   ☐ Masters   ☐ Doctorate

Trade School: (Specify) _____

A HIGH SCHOOL DIPLOMA OR GED EQUIVALENCY IS ACCEPTABLE
VERIFICATION OF EDUCATIONAL ACHIEVEMENT.

FACTOR 3	EXPERIENCE/KNOWLEDGE DESIRED

(Specify type and duration) _MINIMUM EDUCATIONAL ACHIEVEMENT OR 6 MONTHS_
OF PROGRESSIVELY RESPONSIBLE GENERAL WORK EXPERIENCE MAINTAINING
RECORDS, SCREENING, REVIEWING, VERIFYING AND PREPARING DOCUMENTS.

FACTOR 4	LICENSE/CERTIFICATION

Valid Drivers License: ☐ Yes   ☒ No

Other: (Specify) _____

FACTOR 5	PERCEPTION

	PRESENT	NOT PRESENT
SPATIAL:	☐	☒

Ability to comprehend forms in space and understand relationships of plane and solid objects. May be used in such tasks as blueprint reading and in solving geometry problems. Frequently described as the ability to "visualize" objects of two or three dimensions, or to think visually of geometric forms.

	PRESENT	NOT PRESENT
FORM:	☒	☐

Ability to perceive pertinent detail in objects or in pictorial or graphic material. To make visual comparisons and discriminations and see slight differences in shapes and shadings of figures and widths and lengths of line.

	PRESENT	NOT PRESENT
CLERICAL:	☒	☐

Ability to perceive pertinent detail in verbal or tabular material. To observe differences in copy, to proof-read words and numbers, and to avoid perceptual errors in arithmetic computation.

FACTOR 6	DATA

Information, knowledge, and conceptions, related to data, people, or things, obtained by observation, and mental creation. Data is intangible and include numbers, words, symbols, ideas, concepts, and oral verbalization.

	PRESENT	NOT PRESENT
SYNTHESIZING	☐	☒
COORDINATING	☐	☒
ANALYZING	☐	☒
COMPILING	☐	☒
COMPUTING	☐	☒
COPYING	☐	☒
COMPARING.	☒	☐

FACTOR 7	**PEOPLE**

Human beings; also animals dealt with on an individual basis as if they were human.

	PRESENT	NOT PRESENT
MENTORING	☐	☒
NEGOTIATING	☐	☒
INSTRUCTION	☐	☒
SUPERVISING	☐	☒
DIVERTING	☐	☒
PERSUADING	☐	☒
SPEAKING-SIGNALING	☐	☒
SERVING	☐	☒
TAKING INSTRUCTIONS-HELPING	☒	☐

FACTOR 8	**THINGS**

Inanimate objects as distinguished from human beings, substances, or materials; machines, tools, equipment and products. A thing is tangible and has shape, form, and other physical characteristics.

	PRESENT	NOT PRESENT
SETTING UP	☐	☒
PRECISION WORKING	☐	☒
OPERATING-CONTROLLING	☐	☒
DRIVING-OPERATION	☐	☒
MANIPULATING	☐	☒
TENDING	☒	☐
FEEDING-OFFBEARING	☒	☐
HANDLING	☒	☐

ADA–ESSENTIAL FUNCTION IDENTIFICATION

FACTOR 9	PERSONAL TRAITS

Work functions required by specific job-worker situations.

	PRESENT	**NOT PRESENT**

I. ABILITY TO COMPREHEND AND FOLLOW INSTRUCTIONS .... ☒   ❏

The ability to maintain attention and concentration for necessary periods; to apply common sense understanding to carry out instructions furnished in written, oral or diagrammatic form; to adapt to situations requiring the precise attainment of set limits, tolerances or standards; to operate–controls which involve starting, stopping, controlling and adjusting the progress of a machine or piece of equipment.

II. ABILITY TO PERFORM SIMPLE AND REPETITIVE TASKS .... ☒   ❏

The ability to ask simple questions or request assistance; to perform activities of a routine, concrete, organized nature; to remember locations and work procedures; to make decisions based on simple sensory data.

III. ABILITY TO MAINTAIN A WORK PACE APPROPRIATE TO A GIVEN WORK LOAD .... ☒   ❏

The ability to perform activities with a schedule, maintain regular attendance and to be punctual within specified tolerances; to complete a normal work day and/or work week and perform at a consistent pace without unreasonable number and/or length of rest periods; to perform effectively when confronted with potential emergency, critical, unusual or dangerous situations, or in situations in which working speed and sustained attention are make or break aspects of the job (i.e., police work, fire fighter, life guard, crossing guard, security guard, bouncer, body guard, paramedic, emergency room personnel, ICU/CCU nurse, etc.).

IV. ABILITY TO RELATE TO OTHER PEOPLE BEYOND GIVING AND RECEIVING INSTRUCTIONS .... ❏   ☒

The ability to get along with co–workers or peers without exhibiting extreme responses; to perform work activities requiring negotiating with, instructing, supervising, persuading or speaking; to respond appropriately to criticism from a supervisor.

V. ABILITY TO INFLUENCE PEOPLE .... ❏   ☒

The ability to convince or redirect others; to understand the meanings of words and to use them effectively; to interact appropriately with the general public.

VI. ABILITY TO PERFORM COMPLEX OR VARIED TASKS .... ❏   ☒

The ability to synthesize, coordinate and analyze data; to perform jobs requiring precise attainment of set limits, tolerances or standards.

VII. ABILITY TO MAKE GENERALIZATIONS, EVALUATIONS OR DECISIONS WITHOUT IMMEDIATE SUPERVISION .... ❏   ☒

The ability to retain awareness of potential hazards and observe appropriate precautions; to understand and remember detailed instructions; to travel in unfamiliar places or use public transportation systems.

VIII. ABILITY TO ACCEPT AND CARRY OUT RESPONSIBILITY FOR DIRECTION, CONTROL AND PLANNING .... ❏   ☒

The ability to set realistic goals or make plans independently of others; to negotiate with, instruct or supervise people; to respond appropriately to changes in the work setting.

CHAPTER 7

REASONABLE ACCOMMODATION CONSIDERATIONS PER ADA

The legal obligations and methods and types of accommodations are discussed, followed by case studies.

REASONABLE ACCOMMODATION CONSIDERATIONS PER ADA

In the previous chapters we have been primarily discussing methodologies of gathering and documenting job related information. The primary reason for gathering and documenting this information is to assist an employer to determine if an individual applying for an open position or an individual desiring to return to a vacant position is a "Qualified Individual with a Disability" per ADA.

In Chapter 1, we discussed the definition of a qualified individual with a disability. The definition is:

> "Any individual with a disability who satisfies the requisite skill, experience, education and other job related requirements of the employment position such individual holds or desires and who with or without reasonable accommodation can perform the essential functions of such position."

The employer, with knowledge of a need to accommodate can assess whether the qualified individual is able to perform essential functions in the desired position with or without modifications or adjustments. Modifying or adjusting the customary means in which the work is performed is referred to as reasonable accommodations. **Reasonable accommodations is a key nondiscrimination requirement under the ADA.**

Neither the law, interpretive guidance nor the Technical Assistance Manual are as definitive as one would prefer in determining if a proposed accommodation is reasonable or not reasonable. The EEOC definition of reasonable accommodation is:

> "Modifications or adjustments to the job application process, to the work environment or the manner or circumstances under which the position held or desired is customarily performed or; to enable an employee with a disability to enjoy equal benefits and privileges of employment as are enjoyed by other employees without disabilities."

The functional word in *Reasonable Accommodation* is not accommodation but *"Reasonable."* Reasonably accommodating someone is to allow someone to effectively utilize their skills or to enhance skills for the benefit of the employer. With this attitude, you'll find that reasonable accommodation is not just reasonable for the individual with the disability, but also reasonable for the employer, and reasonable for the society as a whole, who cannot afford to allow a valuable human resource to be unutilized through unemployment.

Legal Obligations

The legal obligations of an employer for providing accommodations to an otherwise qualified individual with a disability include the following:

1. An employer must provide reasonable accommodations to the known physical, mental limitations of a qualified applicant or employee with a disability unless it can be shown that the accommodation would impose an undue hardship on the business.

2. The obligation to provide a reasonable accommodation applies to all aspects of employment. This duty is ongoing and may arise anytime that a person's disability or job changes.

3. An employer cannot deny an employment opportunity to a qualified applicant or employee because of the need to provide reasonable accommodation(s), unless it would cause an undue hardship.

4. An employer does not have to make an accommodation for an individual who is not otherwise qualified for the position.

5. It is the obligation of the individual with the disability to request a reasonable accommodation.

6. A qualified individual with a disability has a right to refuse an accommodation. However, if the individual cannot perform the essential functions of the job without the accommodation, he or she may not be qualified for the job.

7. If the cost of an accommodation would impose an undue hardship on the employer the individual with the disability should be given the option of providing the accommodation or personally paying that portion of the cost which would constitute an undue hardship.

EEOC has reinforced that the reasonable accommodation aspect of ADA must be interpreted, considered and implemented on a case-by-case basis. Chris Bell, Assistant Legal Counsel of EEOC, stated in the Federal News Service Bulletin, 1991,

"Every person with a disability has unique abilities and unique limitations, and every job has unique requirements and exist in a unique environment. Accordingly, you can't write a regulation dealing with accommodation in a paint-by-number fashion, so we have not changed the case by case individualized assessment approach."

IDENTIFICATION OF ACCOMMODATIONS

A reasonable accommodation must always take into consideration two unique factors:

1. The specific abilities and functional limitations of a particular applicant or employee with a disability.

2. The specific functional requirements of a particular position.

The process for identifying a reasonable accommodation must begin with the job data of a specific position in which an otherwise qualified individual is making known their mental or physical impairment. An analysis of a particular position would include analyzing the purpose and essential functions of that position. In reference to the initial definition of a qualified individual, the individual must be able to perform the essential functions of the position with or without reasonable accommodations. Without the precise specifications of the job requirements, qualifications and essential functions being known it would be difficult for the employer to analyze which functions require an accommodation to allow the otherwise qualified individual with a disability to perform the function with or without an accommodation. This is a key purpose of having completed job analyses prepared prior to recruitment for an open position.

The individual with the disability must be consulted to find out specifically what his or her physical or mental ability and/or limitations are as they relate to the essential job functions. The physical or mental limitations must be clearly understood as to how they provide a barrier to job performance.

In many situations, the individual with a disability will have already identified potential accommodations and assessed how they might integrate the accommodation into the particular position. The employer would need to consider the potential accommodations and if necessary consult with technical advisors. The effectiveness of each accommodation would need to be assessed. If there are several accommodations that would provide an equal employment opportunity to the individual with the disability, then consider the preference of the individual with the disability and select the accommodation which best serves the needs of the employee and the employer. The employer may choose among effective accommodations and may choose the one which is least expensive or easier to provide. However, if the individual is willing to provide his or her own accommodation the employer may later need to provide the accommodation if for any reason the individual is unable or unwilling to continue to provide their own accommodation.

To adequately evaluate the potential reasonable accommodations the employer must have interactive communications with the disabled person. This process should identify the precise limitations resulting from the disability, identify the potential accommodations that could overcome those limitations to reduce the barriers to employment.

Scope of Accommodations

The ADA requires reasonable accommodations in three aspects of employment:

A. To ensure equal opportunity in the application process.

B. To enable a qualified individual with a disability to perform the essential functions of a job.

C. To enable an employee with a disability to enjoy equal benefits and privileges of employment.

Therefore, the reasonable accommodation question is inclusive of the entire employment process from job seeking, job performance to off-site job training, job travel, employee benefit program eligibility and utilization, job promotions and job transfers. The obligation of the employer is not limited to the individual's performance of the essential functions for one location at one point in time. The employed individual with the disability would need to have access to all privileges of employment as individuals employed by the employer without disabilities would have.

Principles of Accommodation

Remember, that each accommodation must be evaluated on a case-by-case basis. The components of an evaluation include:

- The specific individual with the disability,

- The specific limitations of the individual,

- The essential functions of a specific position, and

- The abilities of an employer in consideration of their financial resources, number of employees, composition and organizational structure.

Some basic principles of reasonable accommodation are:

1. A reasonable accommodation must be an effective accommodation. It must provide an opportunity for a person with a disability to achieve the same level of performance or to enjoy benefits or privileges equal to those of a similarly situated non-disabled person.

2. The reasonable accommodation obligation applies only to accommodations that reduce barriers to employment related to a person's disability. It does not apply to accommodations that a disabled person may request for some other reason.

3. A reasonable accommodation need not be the best accommodation available as long as it is effective for the purpose. It must give the individual with a disability an equal opportunity to be considered for a job, to perform the essential functions of the job, or to enjoy equal benefits and privileges of the job.

4. An employer is not required to provide an accommodation that is primarily for personal use of the individual with the disability. Remember, reasonable accommodations applies to modifications that specifically assist an individual in performing the essential functions of a specific position. Equipment, devices or individuals that assist a disabled person in daily activities outside of the job are considered personal items that an employer is not required to provide.

5. The ADA's requirements for certain types of adjustment and modifications to meet the reasonable accommodation obligation do not prevent an employer from providing accommodations beyond those required by the ADA.

METHODS OF ACCOMMODATIONS

The **job analysis** is critical in the selection of **reasonable accommodations** for individuals with disabilities seeking entry or reentry into the work force. For individuals to be qualified for reasonable accommodations under ADA they need to be able to perform the "essential functions of the position with or without accommodations."

The four most common methods of reasonable accommodation are:

- job restructuring
- job site modifications
- support services
- barrier removal

The need for accommodations is normally a result of an employee or applicant having a **work restriction** that is temporary or permanent. They have a physical, mental or environmental limitation preventing them from performing specific job functions (essential or non-essential) in specific environmental settings. Work restrictions should be determined and recommended by a physician who has reviewed the physical requirements and working conditions of the position. The physician should examine the nature and severity of the medical condition and its importance to the critical abilities required for acceptable job performance. Work restrictions should also be specified as being temporary or permanent for the intended work position.

Work restrictions should be written in a clear and specific language. Frequently the terms "light duty" or "sedentary work" are vague and subject to differing interpretations. For the work restrictions to be meaningful and effective they should convey the same message to management and the individual with the disability. The specific method of reasonable accommodation will depend upon the criticalness of the work restriction to the individual functions of the position held or desired

Job restructuring entails the re-distribution or elimination of marginal duties from a particular position. The position should not be restructured so as not to comply with the job classification for which it was originally defined. Job restructuring should be performed following the completion of a job analysis identifying the specific demands required of the position. In analyzing the position, for job restructuring, the Analyst needs to be observant of those activities which are carried out by a worker due to work habits or for mere worker convenience but may not be a position necessity. To determine the essential from non-essential duties ask, "Would the principal flow of work stop through the elimination of the duty in question." The job analyst may want to discuss examples of job restructuring with the management when performing the job analysis to determine their attitudes and interest in permanent job restructuring to accommodate an individual with a disability.

Job site modifications differ from job restructuring in that these accommodations involve changing the methods and means of task accomplishment. Modifications require creativity, imagination and flexibility on the part of the analyst and management. Job site modifications generally impose some financial costs on the employer. However, these are generally quite small. Many times the disabled individual is the best·source of what modifications may be helpful in them returning to or performing the full capacity of the work.

Per the Job Accommodation Network (JAN), an international information network and consulting resource for accommodating persons with disabilities in the workplace, accommodations are usually not expensive. Per their data, the following table represents the estimated costs and percent of accommodations per dollar category:

31%	No cost
19%	$1 to $50
19%	$51 to $500
19%	$501 to $1,000
11%	$1,001 to $5,000
1%	More than $5,000

Per this data, 50% of the accommodations cost less than $50.00. As my experience has also shown, most accommodations are in the form of job restructuring and minor modifications rather than more costly major modifications, supportive services and architectural barrier removal. JAN provides free accommodation consulting services, call 1-800-526-7234.

In modifying a job site the issues of job performance and eliminating aggravation to the existing medical condition are paramount considerations. The recommendations for purchasing of adaptive equipment or making job site alterations should be based on the ability to return the individual to full job performance. A functional capacity evaluation and/or work hardening program may be necessary to quantify and/or enhance the physical abilities of an individual to perform the job requirements. The Analyst's familiarity with special adaptive tools and equipment is important in recommending and implementing job site modifications. Whenever a modification is implemented, follow up is necessary to ensure the modification is assisting the individual as intended.

Supportive services generally are very difficult to convince an employer to provide or accept as a term of employment. Generally these types of accommodations are utilized in large organizations, major corporations, state and federal agencies. It is most important that the support person hired not perform any of the actual duties of the position in which the disabled person is hired. The support person is to only facilitate job performance, not actually complete job tasks.

Barrier removal is primarily concerned with architectural and institutional barrier removal. Architectural barriers are those that restrict access to facilities and services for individuals with disabilities. Examples of institutional barriers are, employment testing, hiring policies, and selection criterion that screens out disabled individuals from consideration for employment. An example of an institutional barrier removal would be changing the testing procedures to allow the disabled individual to take the test with necessary accommodations (i.e. sign language, reader, an accessible test site).

Regardless of the type of accommodation, the employer should expect the worker's performance to be suitable for the position assigned. The accommodated employee should undergo normal reviews and evaluations for the appraisal of performance as with any other worker. If performance is less than satisfactory then the employer should apply the same corrective action to the situation as to any other employee. **Reasonable accommodation enhances the goals of human resource professionals for the attraction and development of the talents and capabilities of available qualified human resources.**

Types of Accommodation

Some examples of common types of reasonable accommodations that an employer might provide or may find to be appropriate for a particular situation may include:

- Making facilities readily accessible to and usable by individuals with disability

- Restructuring a job by relocating or redistributing marginal job functions

- Altering when and how an essential job function is performed

- Part-time or modified work schedules

- Obtaining or modifying equipment or devices

- Modifying examinations, training materials or policies

- Providing qualified readers and interpreters

- Reassignment to a vacant position

- Permitting use of accrued paid leave or unpaid leave for necessary medical treatments

- Providing reserved parking for a person with a mobility impairment

- Allowing a disabled employee to provide their own equipment or devices that the employer is not required to provide

It is impossible, to list every possible or potential accommodation because a reasonable accommodation must be determined on a case-by-case basis. Remember, a reasonable accommodation must always take into consideration the specific abilities and functional limitations of a particular qualified individual with a disability, and take into consideration the specific functional requirements of a specific position.

Discrimination

Per ADA Title–I, Section 102, discrimination includes:

(5) (A). Not making reasonable accommodations to the known physical or mental limitations of an otherwise qualified individual with a disability who is an applicant or employee, unless such covered entity can demonstrate that the accommodation would impose an undue hardship on the operation of the business of such covered entity; or

(5) (B).   Denying employment opportunities to a job applicant or employee who is otherwise a qualified individual with a disability, if such denial is based on the need of such covered entity to make reasonable accommodation to the physical or mental impairments of the employee or applicant.

Based on the current interpretation of discrimination, the employer has the duty to provide a reasonable accommodation to employees or job applicants when the individuals disability or limitation from performing the job functions have been made known to the employer. The only way employers can escape this responsibility is to demonstrate either that there is no reasonable accommodation, the accommodation poses an undue hardship or the accommodation poses a direct threat.

The employer is required to perform an assessment of the job skills and essential job functions to determine if a reasonable accommodation can be made. If the employer and employee are unable to identify an accommodation or determine what a reasonable accommodation may be, then a specialist; such as a Vocational Rehabilitation Specialist, Physical Therapist or Occupational Therapist may be appropriate to provide an evaluation and recommendations.

Per the EEOC Technical Assistance Manual, the proposed accommodation should be an "effective accommodation" as it should enable the disabled individual to perform the essential functions of the position with equal benefits and opportunities of employment. An employer may decide not to provide a reasonable accommodation because it is felt that it would be an undue hardship to do so.

UNDUE HARDSHIP

Per the ADA Title–I, an undue hardship may result when a recommended accommodation entails significant difficulty or expense to provide. It is defined in the law as:

"Undue Hardship"

(A).   In general the term undue hardship means an action requiring significant difficulty or expense, when considered in light of the factors set forth in sub-paragraph B.

(B).   Factors to be considered. In determining whether an accommodation would impose an undue hardship on a covered entity, factors to be considered include:

    1.   The nature and cost of the accommodation needed under the Act;

2. The overall financial resources of the facility or facilities involved in a provision of the reasonable accommodation; the number of persons employed in such facility; the effect on expenses and resources, or the impact otherwise of such accommodation upon the operation of the facility;

3. The overall financial resources of the covered entity. The overall size of the business of a covered entity with respect to the number of employees; the number, type, and location of its facility or facilities; and

4. The type of operations of the covered entity including the composition, structure and functions of the work force of such entity; the geographic separateness, administrative or physical relationship of the facility or facilities in question to the covered entity.

Per the interpretive guidelines, undue hardship is considered a **defense** against charges of not making reasonable accommodations. The definition of undue hardship is such that what specifically constitutes an undue hardship is not explicitly stated. There are a number of factors which must be taken into consideration when analyzing if an accommodation would bring about an undue hardship upon a given employer. Through case law, no doubt, undue hardship will be further defined. The undue hardship factors to consider will hopefully be further prioritized to assist in future considerations and determinations of proposed accommodations.

LET'S SEE IT WORK

The legal obligations of employers per ADA were discussed in detail in Chapters 1 and 7. The methodologies of identifying and documenting essential functions, qualifications and requirements were discussed in Chapters 2, 3, 4, 5 and 6. Following are two case studies to further demonstrate the interactive application of these legal mandates and data gathering methodologies.

CASE STUDY 1

In the Introduction you met Ms. Evans, the Human Resource Manager. She has been notified by an employee that an accommodation will be required to permit the employee to return to work and perform the essential functions of the desired position. Ms. Evans is unsure how to evaluate the position and employee to determine reasonable accommodations which will facilitate the employee's return to work.

QUESTIONS

1. Is Ms. Evans legally required to evaluate the employees request for reasonable accommodations?

2. What information does Ms. Evans have to gather to initially evaluate what accommodations may be reasonable to provide?

3. For what reason(s) would Ms. Evans not have to provide reasonable accommodations?

ANSWERS

1. Yes, Ms. Evans' company is required to evaluate the possibility of providing reasonable accommodations for the following reasons:

    A) There are more than 25 employees,

    B) The employee is a qualified individual with a disability (the employee had previously performed the functions),

    C) The employer now has knowledge of the need for accommodating, and

    D) The desired position is vacant.

2. Ms. Evans would best be served with the following data:

    A) A Job Analysis specifying the essential functions and job requirements of the position.

    B) Documentation clearly specifying the medical impairments in terms of work restrictions.

    C) An interactive discussion with the employee regarding the accommodations desired or being requested for consideration of their reasonableness and ability to permit the employee to carry out the essential functions of the position.

3. Ms. Evans could choose not to provide accommodations for the following reasons:

A) Effective accommodations would not facilitate the employees' ability to perform the essential functions.

B) The accommodation(s) is (are) for the personal use of the employee and not a job related requirement.

C) The accommodation(s) would be an undue hardship upon the employer due to the limited financial resources and limited staffing available to redistribute marginal functions.

Case Study 2

In the Introduction, you met Mr. Williams, a 42 year old Warehouseman, who works in the shipping department of a mid-size manufacturer. Following a four month medical leave of absence for a lower back strain, he is requesting to return to the position he previously had which is still vacant. Mr. Williams has been medically released to return to work with the permanent restrictions of; no repetitive lifting of heavy objects (more than 50 pounds) and from repetitive bending and stooping activities.

The original employer prepared job description, completed job analysis worksheet and new job description of Mr. Williams' position are at the end of Chapter 6. Turn to Chapter 6 and review these documents.

Questions

1. What are the three criteria which must precede an employers evaluation for accommodating an employee? Have the criteria been met in this case study?

2. What are the four steps of evaluating a position for consideration of implementing reasonable accommodations?

3. What are some examples of reasonable accommodations which would enable Mr. Williams to return to work as a warehouse worker?

Answers

1. A) The employer must verify that the individual with the disability is a qualified individual with a disability.

   B) The limitations have to have been disclosed to the employer.

C) There must be a vacant position.

   The criteria has been established in this case study. The employer must evaluate the possibility of accommodating Mr. Williams.

2. A) The gathering of position specific data including essential functions, requirements and qualifications.

   B) An interactive process including the qualified individual with a disability to clarify limitations and their impact on performance of essential functions and identification of suggested accommodations for the individual.

   C) An evaluation of the effectiveness of all the considered accommodations.

   D) Determine if the accommodation is an "Undue Hardship," if not, offer the position and the accommodation to the individual.

3. A) Train Mr. Williams in proper lifting techniques to minimize his trunk bending and encourage him to kneel or squat more frequently with his back straight. Consider offering a back brace for Mr. Williams and co-workers to encourage proper body mechanics.

   B) Construct a platform along the conveyor to raise the cargo up off the floor to minimize bending, stooping and lifting from the below knee level up to 35" high conveyor.

   C) Instruct department workers to jointly lift items weighing in excess of 50 pounds.

   D) Encourage workers to utilize cargo handling equipment such as two wheel dollies, pallet jacks and forklifts to minimize bending, lifting and carry requirements.

   E) Integrate employee performance evaluations and proper cargo handling techniques to enhance responsibility by supervisors and employees for utilizing accommodations.

APPENDIX A

SAMPLE EMPLOYER JOB DESCRIPTIONS

- CONSTRUCTION TRADES
- TRUCK DRIVER, SEMI
- CUSTODIAN I

South Madison Unified School District

CONSTRUCTION TRADES

CARPENTER - ELECTRICIAN - GLAZIER - HEATING, VENTILATING -AIR CONDITIONING - LOCKSMITH - MASONRY - PAINTER - PLUMBER - WELDER

DEFINITION

Under general supervision, performs skilled journeyman duties in one of the building trades, new construction, repairs of facilities and furnishings, maintenance, and performs other duties as assigned.

TYPICAL TASKS

Performs skilled journeyman duties in one of the following trade fields, assisting others in related tasks as required:

CARPENTER—The Trades I Carpenter performs journeyman new and maintenance carpentry work including rough and finished construction in connection with repair and remodeling jobs; builds cupboards and counters; installs partitions, repairs furniture; hangs doors; installs and replaces related building hardware.

ELECTRICIAN—The Trades I Electrician performs journeyman level work installing new wiring, leads, fixtures; maintains and repairs electrical wiring system and equipment such as motors, starting equipment, switchboards, lighting equipment, etc.; locates trouble in wiring and electrical equipment and makes repairs; replaces defective equipment and wiring; replaces and repairs equipment such as motor-driven appliances, extension cords, central clock systems, public-address system; works from blueprints and wiring diagrams; is familiar with electrical standards and codes.

GLAZIER—The Trades I Glazier performs journeyman level work with installation and/or replacement of all types of glazing materials. Estimates costs of these installations and orders glazing materials as needed. Also works with carpenters and locksmiths on related problems with doors, windows, door closers and associated hardware.

HEATING, VENTILATING, AIR CONDITIONING—The Trades I specialist with Heating, Ventilating, Air Conditioning does skilled journeyman installations of new and replacement units and parts of air conditioning and refrigeration equipment lines, power source and controls; charges systems with coolant gases; inspects cooling towers, controls and lines for damage and leaks; maintains and repairs all related equipment; is familiar with heating, refrigeration and electrical standards and codes.

LOCKSMITH—The Trades I Locksmith maintains master key file for all district facilities, cuts new keys as required, changes key combinations as necessary, installs and repairs door closers. In addition, the Locksmith is a member of the District Security Team.

MASONRY—The Trades I specialist with Masonry performs skilled journeyman installation of concrete retaining walls, sidewalks, planter boxes, decks and patios. Does similar installations involving brick, rock, flagstone and other similar building materials. Also supervises unskilled and semi-skilled personnel in these installations.

PAINTER—The Trades I Painter performs journeyman level work in outside and inside painting of new and old buildings, structures and equipment; mixes paints and matches colors; cleans, sands, putties and patches surfaces, and otherwise prepares surfaces for painting, uses brushes, roller, spray gun to apply paint; may erect and work from scaffold.

PLUMBER—The Trades I Plumber performs journeyman tasks installing, maintaining and repairing sanitary plumbing pipes and fixtures, and air, oil and gas pipes and heating systems; bends, cuts, rems and threads pipes; tests joints and pipe systems for leaks; is familiar with plumbing standards and codes.

POLICY STANDARDS—TRADES

TRADES I— An all-around journeyman in one of the building trades; does not include handyman, utilityman or apprentices.

EMPLOYMENT STANDARDS

KNOWLEDGE— Knowledge of methods, tools, equipment materials and means of transportation for the particular journeyman tasks.

ABILITY—Ability to read blueprints, estimate time and material for job orders; ability to train and direct efforts of others effectively. Should have ability to drive a light truck or van to and from jobs; ability to perform in the official absence of the Trades II in the same field.

EXPERIENCE—Evidence of successful experience as an apprentice or helper under the supervision and training of a skilled journeyman in the same field.

EDUCATION—Graduation from high school or recognized trade school, or completion of equivalent training and experience.

Must possess a valid driver's license. Must have a good driving record. Insurable under the district's insurance program and must maintain insurability.

Coastal Warehouse

JOB DESCRIPTION

LABOR GRADE: MB

TRUCK DRIVER - SEMI

OCCUPATIONAL SUMMARY

This occupation requires the driving, loading and unloading of semi-tractors and semi-trailers on and off company property.

WORK PERFORMED

Drives semi-tractors and semi-trailers of any capacity for intra-plant and off-site company hauling. Makes pickups at and deliveries to depots, freight terminals, stores, warehouses and other designated locations as dispatched. Loads or cooperates with others in loading materials, salvage, parts, assemblies, tooling and equipment. Checks against written instructions or follows verbal orders, responsible for the checking of load for safety and correctness of loading procedure prior to movement, delivers to proper destination and unloads or cooperates with others when unloading. Checks pickups and deliveries against shipping documents and handles all necessary paperwork. Obtains required driver's licenses.

Does emergency roadside maintenance work such as repairing tubes and changing tires, light bulbs, fuses and plugs when necessary.

Initiate and assure corrective action to restore vehicles to proper operation efficiency and maintain cleanliness of assigned vehicle.

6-31-69
4-3-72—Reviewed - No change
4-7-75—Reviewed - No change
4-24-78—Reviewed - No change

Aztec Towers, Inc.

Class Title: Custodian I

Unit Designation: Operations

Title: Class Description

Date: 8/83

Page: 1 **of** 2

DEFINITION

Under the direction of a Crew Leader, Custodial Supervisor or other supervisor, maintain assigned area such as classrooms, offices and buildings in a clean, safe and orderly manner.

DISTINGUISHING CHARACTERISTICS

Incumbents in this class perform the full range of custodial duties involved in cleaning and maintaining assigned areas. The Custodian II classification performs a full range of custodial duties plus light repair and maintenance activities, the latter comprising at least 50% of the work day.

EXAMPLE OF DUTIES

1. Sweep, scrub, mop, wax, oil and buff floors; vacuum and shampoo rugs and carpets; operate equipment such as floor buffers nd vacuum cleaners.

2. Clean and disinfect lavatories, toilets and other plumbing fixtures; wash windows; dust, wax and polish furniture and woodwork.

3. Set up furniture and equipment for meetings and events; rearrange furniture and equipment as required; direct visitors.

4. Clean chalkboards; refill paper and other sanitary dispensers; empty and clean waste containers.

5. Replace light bulbs; raise and lower flag; turn out lights and lock doors.

6. Open school facilities; inspect doors, windows, locks and equipment to assure security; safeguard property.

7. Report sanitary and safety hazards to the proper authorities.

8. Pick up paper and other refuse from grounds; sweep walkways and outside areas.

9. May assist in receiving, storing and inventorying supplies as assigned or in the absence of the supervisor.

10. Perform related duties as assigned.

Custodian I – continued

DESIRABLE QUALIFICATIONS

KNOWLEDGE:

Cleaning materials, disinfectants and equipment utilized.

Methods of cleaning and preserving floors, furniture, walls and fixtures.

Health and safety regulations.

Common tools and their names.

SKILLS AND ABILITIES:

Perform heavy physical labor.

Utilize cleaning materials and equipment efficiently.

Understand and follow oral and written directions.

Work cooperatively with others.

TRAINING AND EXPERIENCE:

Any combination of training and experience equivalent to sufficient training and experience to demonstrate the knowledge and abilities listed above.

LICENSE:

Valid driver's license.

WORKING CONDITIONS

PHYSICAL REQUIREMENTS

Category I

ENVIRONMENT:

Inside, subject to fumes, odors, toxic conditions and dust; work with cleaning chemicals.

SAMPLE
ESSENTIAL FUNCTIONS–
DEMANDS JOB ANALYSIS
WORKSHEETS

- CONSTRUCTION TRADES
- TRUCK DRIVER, SEMI
- CUSTODIAN I

ESSENTIAL FUNCTIONS–DEMANDS JOB ANALYSIS WORKSHEET

Date _11-4-92_   Job Analyst _R. THRUSH_

JOB INFORMATION

Title _PAINTER_   Employer _SOUTH MADISON UNIFIED SCHOOL DISTRICT_

Job Code _872_   Labor Grade _MT-I_   Salary/Rate _$2375 PER MONTH_

Department _PAINTING_   Shift Assignment: A _____ B _X_ C _____

Work Unit _SPECIALTY CREW_   Number Of Employees _1_

Union Affiliation _NONE_

Supervisor(s) _____   Phone No(s). _____
BRUCE STONE   _213-7300 EXT. 024_

Incumbent(s) _____   Badge/SSN _____
JOE BEAN   _262-11-8719_

Job Description: Reviewed_____   To Update _____   Not-Available_____

JOB SUMMARY

Reason the position exists (purpose):

The purpose of this position is to _APPLY PAINT TO STREETS, PARKING, PLAYGROUND, INSTRUCTIONAL AREAS AND STRUCTURES._

Production or Workload

ESTIMATED LABOR HOURS PER LABOR MANUAL GUIDELINES.

JOB FUNCTIONS

Essential Functions: Identify the critical duties actually performed by incumbents to fulfill the purpose of this position.

Write in prescribed sentence structure: action verb, object, [to] outcome, using M, E, T, W/A (machines, equipment, etc.).

Mark the "critical" box if not performing the duty would interrupt the flow of work. Include the daily % of time spent performing the critical duties. May not equal 100% due to performance of marginal duties.

DAILY % TIME	CRITICAL	ACTION VERB	OBJECT	[TO] OUTCOME/METW/A
10%	✔	*Reads*	*Instructions*	*To complete the form*
15%	✔	DETERMINES	PAINTING OPERATIONS	TO COMPLY WITH WRITTEN AND VERBAL INSTRUCTIONS AND TRADE PRACTICES
40%	✔	PREPARES	PAINTING SURFACES	TO ENSURE ADHESION OF PRIMER AND FINISH COATS OF PAINT USING
				SCRAPERS, ELECTRIC SANDERS AND CLEANING SURFACES.
30%	✔	APPLIES	PAINT	TO METAL, WOOD, BRICK, CONCRETE, DRYWALL AND ASPHALT SURFACES
				USING HAND ROLLER, BRUSH, AIRLESS SPRAY PAINT APPARATUS AND
				STRIPPING MACHINE.
5%	✔	SETS UP	LADDERS & SCAFFOLDING	TO ENSURE SAFE ABOVE GROUND WORK PLATFORM.
		INVENTORIES	PAINT SUPPLIES	TO MAINTAIN SUFFICIENT SUPPLY.
5%	✔	DRIVES	CREW VEHICLE	TO TRANSPORT CREW, EQUIPMENT AND SUPPLIES TO THE JOB SITE.

ESSENTIAL FUNCTIONS CRITERIA CHECKLIST

POSITION TITLE: _PAINTER_

FUNCTION: _DETERMINES PAINTING OPERATIONS TO COMPLY WITH_
WRITTEN AND VERBAL INSTRUCTIONS AND TRADE PRACTICES

(Complete a checklist for each function)

PRIMARY CONSIDERATIONS	YES	NO
1. Do incumbents actually perform the function?	☒	❏
2. Would removing the function fundamentally change the position?	☒	❏

REASONS TO CONSIDER	YES	NO
1. Does the position exist to perform the function?	☒	❏
2. Are there a limited number of employees who could perform the function?	☒	❏
3. Are the functions highly specialized?	❏	☒

EVIDENCE TO CONSIDER	YES	NO
1. Employers judgement that the function is essential?	☒	❏
2. Does a written Job Description include the function?	❏	☒
3. Is there a significant amount of time spent performing the function?	☒	❏
4. Are there serious consequences in not performing the function?	☒	❏
5. Is there a Collective Bargaining Agreement?	❏	☒

Function is Essential:	☒	❏

Analyst Name ___R. THRUSH___ Date ___11-4-92___

Incumbent's Name ___J. BEAN___ Date ___11-4-92___

Supervisor Name ___B.STONE___ Date ___11-4-92___

ORGANIZATIONAL RELATIONSHIPS

Identify as specifically as possible the relationship of the assigned work unit to the department and to the organization as a whole. Briefly state the overall purpose of the work unit and/or department to the organization. Sketch an organizational flowchart of the relationship of the work unit and/or department to the nearest related work units or departments.

Identify as specifically as possible the specific names and titles of the people who report to this position, and the name and title who this position reports to.

```
        ┌─────────────────────────┐
        │   FACILITY MAINTENANCE   │
        │        DIRECTOR          │
        └─────────────────────────┘
                    │
            ┌───────────────┐
            │ TRADE MANAGERS │
            └───────────────┘
          │
    ┌──────────────────┐
    │ PAINTING FOREMAN │
    └──────────────────┘
          │
    ┌──────────────────┐
    │    SPECIALTY     │
    │   CREW LEADER    │
    └──────────────────┘
          │
    ┌──────────────────┐
    │    INCUMBENT     │
    └──────────────────┘
```

JOB REQUIREMENTS

PHYSICAL FACTORS

KEY: NP = Not Present   O = 1/3 of the day
F = 1/3–2/3 of the day   C = Over 2/3 of the day

FACTOR 1:   STRENGTH

MOBILITY   **FREQUENCY**

			NP	O	F	C
A.	Stand _30_ % of time _2.5_ hrs/day		☐	☒	☐	☐
B.	Walk _50_ % of time _4.0_ hrs/day		☐	☐	☒	☐
C.	Sit _20_ % of time _1.5_ hrs/day		☐	☒	☐	☐

_100%_   _4/8/10_ hrs/day

COMMENTS: _____

LIFTING   **FREQUENCY**

	NP	O	F	C
up to 5 lbs	☐	☐	☐	☒
6 - 10 lbs	☐	☐	☐	☒
11 - 20 lbs	☐	☐	☒	☐
21 - 25 lbs	☐	☐	☒	☐
26 - 50 lbs	☐	☒	☐	☐
51 - 75 lbs	☐	☒	☐	☐
76 - 100 lbs	☒	☐	☐	☐
Over 100 lbs	☒	☐	☐	☐

COMMENTS: (Heaviest item and range of vertical distance) _____
A FIVE GALLON CAN OF PAINT WEIGHS 60 TO 75 POUNDS AND MAY BE LIFTED UP TO WAIST HEIGHT.

FACTOR 1: STRENGTH — Continued

CARRYING — FREQUENCY

	NP	O	F	C
up to 5 lbs	☐	☐	☐	☒
6 - 10 lbs	☐	☐	☐	☒
11 - 20 lbs	☐	☐	☐	☒
21 - 25 lbs	☐	☒	☐	☐
26 - 50 lbs	☐	☒	☐	☐
51 - 75 lbs	☐	☒	☐	☐
76 - 100 lbs	☒	☐	☐	☐
Over 100 lbs	☒	☐	☐	☐

COMMENTS: (Heaviest item and range of horizontal distance) _A FIVE GALLON CAN OF PAINT WEIGHING 60 TO 75 POUNDS MAY BE CARREID IN ONE HAND A MAXIMUM OF 150 FEET._

PUSHING/PULLING — FREQUENCY

	NP	O	F	C
5 lbs	☐	☐	☐	☒
6 - 10 lbs	☐	☐	☐	☒
11 - 20 lbs	☒	☐	☐	☐
21 - 25 lbs	☒	☐	☐	☐
26 - 50 lbs	☒	☐	☐	☐
51 - 75 lbs	☐	☐	☒	☐
76 - 100 lbs	☒	☐	☐	☐
Over 100 lbs	☒	☐	☐	☐

COMMENTS: (Wheeled objects, Footpedal, Lever, Equipment or Hand tool) _PUSHES WHEELED STRIPPING MACHINE WEIGHING UP TO 75 POUNDS TO APPLY PAINT TO ASHPALT SURFACES. REPETITIVELY PUSHES AND PULLS TO USE HAND AND ROLLER BRUSHES TO PAINT._

FACTOR 2: AGILITY

FREQUENCY

		NP	O	F	C
A.	Climbing	☐	☒	☐	☐
B.	Balancing	☐	☒	☐	☐
C.	Bending	☐	☐	☐	☒
D.	Stooping	☐	☐	☐	☒
E.	Crouching	☐	☐	☐	☒
F.	Kneeling	☐	☐	☒	☐

FACTOR 2: AGILITY Continued

FREQUENCY

			NP	O	F	C
G.	Crawling		☐	☒	☐	☐
H.	Running		☒	☐	☐	☐
I.	Twisting		☐	☒	☐	☐
J.	Turning		☐	☒	☐	☐
K.	Jumping		☒	☐	☐	☐

COMMENTS: _____

_____

_____

FACTOR 3: DEXTERITY

FREQUENCY

			NP	O	F	C
A.	Grasping–Firm/Strong		☐	☐	☐	☒
B.	Finger Dexterity		☐	☒	☐	☐
C.	Reaching Forward		☐	☐	☐	☒
D.	Reaching Overhead		☐	☒	☐	☐
E.	Pinching		☐	☒	☐	☐
F.	Grasping–Light		☒	☐	☐	☐

Dominant hand: ☒ Right ☐ Left ☐ Both

COMMENTS: _TO GRASP PAINTING BRUSH/ROLLER, TO PUSH STRIPPING MACHINE, TO USE_
PAINT SPRAY EQUIPMENT.

FACTOR 4: COORDINATION

FREQUENCY

			NP	O	F	C
A.	Eye - hand		☐	☐	☐	☒
B.	Eye - Hand - Foot		☐	☒	☐	☐
C.	Driving		☐	☒	☐	☐

COMMENTS: _TO DRIVE COMPANY VEHICLE TO JOB SITE._

FACTOR 5: VISION

		NP	O	F	C
A.	Acuity, Near	☐	☐	☐	☒
B.	Acuity, Far	☐	☐	☐	☒
C.	Depth Perception	☒	☐	☐	☐
D.	Accommodation	☒	☐	☐	☐
E.	Color Vision	☐	☒	☐	☐
F.	Field of Vision	☒	☐	☐	☐

COMMENTS: _____

_____

_____

FACTOR 6: TALKING

		NP	O	F	C
A.	Face-to-Face Contact	☐	☒	☐	☐
B.	Verbal Contact with Others	☐	☒	☐	☐
C.	Public	☐	☐	☒	☐

COMMENTS: _WORKS AT ELEMENTARY SCHOOL SITES OFTEN WITH SCHOOL IN SESSION._
COMMUNICATES WITH PARENTS, CHILDREN, PRINCIPALS, TEACHERS AND CO-WORKERS.

_____

FACTOR 7: HEARING

		NP	O	F	C
A.	Normal Conversation	☐	☐	☒	☐
B.	Telephone Communication	☐	☒	☐	☐
C.	Earplugs Required	☐	☒	☐	☐

COMMENTS: _____

_____

_____

ENVIRONMENTAL FACTORS

		NP	O	F	C
A.	Works indoors	☐	☒	☐	☐
B.	Works outdoors	☐	☐	☐	☒
C.	Exposure to extreme hot or cold temperature	☒	☐	☐	☐
D.	Working at unprotected heights	☒	☐	☐	☐
E.	Being around moving machinery	☒	☐	☐	☐
F.	Exposure to marked changes in temperature/humidity	☐	☒	☐	☐
G.	Exposure to dust, fumes, smoke, gases, odors, mists or other irritating particles	☐	☐	☒	☐
	(specify) _____				
H.	Exposure to toxic or caustic chemicals	☐	☒	☐	☐
I.	Exposure to excessive noises	☐	☒	☐	☐
J.	Exposure to radiation or electrical energy	☒	☐	☐	☐
K.	Exposure to solvents, grease, or oils	☐	☒	☐	☐
L.	Exposure to slippery or uneven walking surfaces	☐	☒	☐	☐
M.	Working below ground	☒	☐	☐	☐
N.	Using computer (CRT) monitor	☒	☐	☐	☐
O.	Working with explosives	☒	☐	☐	☐
P.	Exposure to vibration	☐	☒	☐	☐
Q.	Exposure to flames or burning items	☒	☐	☐	☐
R.	Works around others	☐	☐	☐	☒
S.	Works alone	☐	☐	☐	☒
T.	Works with others	☐	☒	☐	☐

COMMENTS: (Describe special conditions) *EXPOSED TO PAINT FUMES WORKING OUTDOORS AND INDOORS AND OTHER FUMES OR TO DUST REQUIRING USE OF CARBON CARTRIDGE 3/4 FACE RESPIRATOR OR PAPER INHALATION MASK.*

SAFETY FACTORS

	PRESENT	NOT PRESENT
Material Safety Data Sheets		
(Verify Availability and Current)	☒	☐
Safety Equipment (Required to Wear)		
Safety Glasses	☐	☒
Ear Plugs	☒	☐
Hard Hat	☐	☒
Protective Clothing	☒	☐
Other *CARBON CARTRIDGE RESPIRATOR*	☒	☐
FULL FACE SHIELD/PAPER INHALER MASK	☒	☐

MACHINES • EQUIPMENT • TOOLS • WORK AIDS

MACHINES

Devices which are a combination of mechanical parts, power actuated and designed to apply force to do work on or move materials or to process data. Vehicles are considered to be machines.

List	Skilled	OJT
CREW TRUCK – AUTOMATIC	☐	☒
MIXER	☐	☒
AIRLESS SPRAYER	☒	☐
STRIPPING MACHINE	☐	☒
	☐	☐
	☐	☐
	☐	☐
	☐	☐
	☐	☐
	☐	☐

EQUIPMENT

Devices which are power actuated and generally designed to be portable and used to apply a force to do work on or move material or to process data.

List	Skilled	OJT
DRILL MOTOR MIXER	☒	☐
ORBITAL SANDER	☒	☐
	☐	☐
	☐	☐
	☐	☐
	☐	☐
	☐	☐
	☐	☐
	☐	☐
	☐	☐

MACHINES • EQUIPMENT • TOOLS • WORK AIDS

TOOLS

Devices or implements which are not power actuated and are manipulated by hand to do work on or move materials.

LIST	SKILLED	OJT
SCRAPER, WIRE BRUSH, PUTTY KNIFE	☒	☐
PAINT BRUSH, ROLLERS	☒	☐
LADDERS, STEP AND EXTENSION	☒	☐
PORTABLE SCAFFOLDING	☐	☒
HANDTOOLS, MEASURING TAPE	☒	☐
	☐	☐
	☐	☐
	☐	☐
	☐	☐
	☐	☐

WORK AIDS

Items not considered to be a machine, equipment or tool yet are necessary for carrying out the work.

LIST	SKILLED	OJT
MASKING TAPE, PAPER, PLASTIC	☒	☐
STENCILS	☐	☒
	☐	☐
	☐	☐
	☐	☐
	☐	☐
	☐	☐
	☐	☐
	☐	☐
	☐	☐

KEY

OJT– The worker will need to learn to use upon commencing work in the position

SKILLED– The worker would need to have experience prior to commencing work in the position

JOB QUALIFICATIONS

MENTAL FACTORS

FACTOR 1   GENERAL EDUCATION DEVELOPMENT

REASONING	PRESENT	NOT PRESENT
Deal with abstract and concrete variables, define problems, collect data, establish facts, and draw valid conclusions	☐	☒
Interpret instructions furnished in written, oral, diagrammatic, or schedule form..	☒	☐
Deal with problems from standard situations	☒	☐
Carry out detailed but uninvolved written or oral instructions............	☒	☐
Carry out single one or two step instructions	☒	☐

MATHEMATICS	PRESENT	NOT PRESENT
COMPLEX SKILLS Business math, algebra, geometry, shopmath or statistics..	☒	☐
SIMPLE SKILLS Add, subtract, multiply and divide whole numbers and fractions, make change, calculate time, calculate simple measurements	☐	☐

READING	PRESENT	NOT PRESENT
COMPLEX SKILLS Comprehend newspapers, manuals, journals, instructions in use and maintenance of shop tools and equipment, safety rules and procedures and drawings...........................	☒	☐
SIMPLE SKILLS English at the 6th grade level (tested), comprehend simple instructions or notations from a log book	☐	☐

FACTOR 1 — GENERAL EDUCATION DEVELOPMENT — continued

WRITING   PRESENT   NOT PRESENT

COMPLEX SKILLS

Prepare business letters, summaries of reports using
prescribed format and conforming to all rules of spelling,
punctuation, grammar, diction and style .... ☐   ☒

SIMPLE SKILLS

English sentences containing subject, verb and object;
names and addresses, complete job application or
notations in a log book .... ☒   ☐

FACTOR 2 — EDUCATIONAL ACHIEVEMENT

High School: ☒ Yes ☐ No

College Degree: ☐ Associate ☐ Bachelor ☐ Masters ☐ Doctorate

Trade School: (Specify) _____

_____

_____

_____

_____

_____

FACTOR 3 — EXPERIENCE/KNOWLEDGE DESIRED

(Specify type and duration) *KNOWLEDGE OF METHODS, TOOLS, EQUIPMENT, MATERIALS AND
MEANS OF PAINTING. ABILITY TO READ BLUEPRINTS AND ESTIMATE MATERIALS REQUIRED
FOR ORDERS. A MINIMUM OF TWO YEARS EXPERIENCE UNDER JOURNEYMAN PAINTER.*

_____

_____

_____

FACTOR 4 — LICENSE/CERTIFICATION

Valid Drivers License: ☒ Yes ☐ No

Other: (Specify) *GOOD DRIVING RECORD. INSURABLE.*

_____

_____

_____

_____

FACTOR 5 — PERCEPTION

	PRESENT	NOT PRESENT
SPATIAL:	☒	☐

Ability to comprehend forms in space and understand relationships of plane and solid objects. May be used in such tasks as blueprint reading and in solving geometry problems. Frequently described as the ability to "visualize" objects of two or three dimensions, or to think visually of geometric forms.

	PRESENT	NOT PRESENT
FORM:	☒	☐

Ability to perceive pertinent detail in objects or in pictorial or graphic material. To make visual comparisons and discriminations and see slight differences in shapes and shadings of figures and widths and lengths of line.

	PRESENT	NOT PRESENT
CLERICAL:	☐	☒

Ability to perceive pertinent detail in verbal or tabular material. To observe differences in copy, to proof-read words and numbers, and to avoid perceptual errors in arithmetic computation.

FACTOR 6 — DATA

Information, knowledge, and conceptions, related to data, people, or things, obtained by observation, and mental creation. Data are intangible and include numbers, words, symbols, ideas, concepts, and oral verbalization.

	PRESENT	NOT PRESENT
SYNTHESIZING	☐	☒
COORDINATING	☒	☐
ANALYZING	☒	☐
COMPILING	☐	☒
COMPUTING	☒	☐
COPYING	☐	☒
COMPARING.	☒	☐

FACTOR 7   PEOPLE

Human beings; also animals dealt with on an individual basis as if they were human.

	PRESENT	NOT PRESENT
MENTORING	❏	☒
NEGOTIATING	❏	☒
INSTRUCTION	❏	☒
SUPERVISING	❏	☒
DIVERTING	❏	☒
PERSUADING	❏	☒
SPEAKING-SIGNALING	☒	❏
SERVING	☒	❏
TAKING INSTRUCTIONS-HELPING	☒	❏

FACTOR 8   THINGS

Inanimate objects as distinguished from human beings, substances, or materials; machines, tools, equipment and products. A thing is tangible and has shape, form, and other physical characteristics.

	PRESENT	NOT PRESENT
SETTING UP	☒	❏
PRECISION WORKING	☒	❏
OPERATING-CONTROLLING	☒	❏
DRIVING-OPERATION	☒	❏
MANIPULATING	☒	❏
TENDING	☒	❏
FEEDING-OFFBEARING	☒	❏
HANDLING	☒	❏

ADA–Essential Function Identification

FACTOR 9	PERSONAL TRAITS

Work functions required by specific job-worker situations.

	PRESENT	NOT PRESENT

I. ABILITY TO COMPREHEND AND FOLLOW INSTRUCTIONS .... ☒ ❏

The ability to maintain attention and concentration for necessary periods; to apply common sense understanding to carry out instructions furnished in written, oral or diagrammatic form; to adapt to situations requiring the precise attainment of set limits, tolerances or standards; to operate–controls which involve starting, stopping, controlling and adjusting the progress of a machine or piece of equipment.

II. ABILITY TO PERFORM SIMPLE AND REPETITIVE TASKS .... ☒ ❏

The ability to ask simple questions or request assistance; to perform activities of a routine, concrete, organized nature; to remember locations and work procedures; to make decisions based on simple sensory data.

III. ABILITY TO MAINTAIN A WORK PACE APPROPRIATE TO A GIVEN WORK LOAD .... ☒ ❏

The ability to perform activities with a schedule, maintain regular attendance and to be punctual within specified tolerances; to complete a normal work day and/or work week and perform at a consistent pace without unreasonable number and/or length of rest periods; to perform effectively when confronted with potential emergency, critical, unusual or dangerous situations, or in situations in which working speed and sustained attention are make or break aspects of the job (i.e., police work, fire fighter, life guard, crossing guard, security guard, bouncer, body guard, paramedic, emergency room personnel, ICU/CCU nurse, etc.

IV. ABILITY TO RELATE TO OTHER PEOPLE BEYOND GIVING AND RECEIVING INSTRUCTIONS .... ☒ ❏

The ability to get along with co–workers or peers without exhibiting extreme responses; to perform work activities requiring negotiating with, instructing, supervising, persuading or speaking; to respond appropriately to criticism from a supervisor.

V. ABILITY TO INFLUENCE PEOPLE .... ☒ ❏

The ability to convince or redirect others; to understand the meanings of words and to use them effectively; to interact appropriately with the general public.

VI. ABILITY TO PERFORM COMPLEX OR VARIED TASKS .... ☒ ❏

The ability to synthesize, coordinate and analyze data; to perform jobs requiring precise attainment of set limits, tolerances or standards.

VII. ABILITY TO MAKE GENERALIZATIONS, EVALUATIONS OR DECISIONS WITHOUT IMMEDIATE SUPERVISION .... ☒ ❏

The ability to retain awareness of potential hazards and observe appropriate precautions; to understand and remember detailed instructions; to travel in unfamiliar places or use public transportation systems.

VIII. ABILITY TO ACCEPT AND CARRY OUT RESPONSIBILITY FOR DIRECTION, CONTROL AND PLANNING .... ☒ ❏

The ability to set realistic goals or make plans independently of others; to negotiate with , instruct or supervise people; to respond appropriately to changes in the work setting.

ESSENTIAL FUNCTIONS–DEMANDS JOB ANALYSIS WORKSHEET

Date _6-26-92_   Job Analyst _R. THRUSH_

JOB INFORMATION

Title _TRUCK DRIVER_   Employer _COASTAL WAREHOUSE_

Job Code _985_   Labor Grade _MB_   Salary/Rate _$2166 PER MONTH_

Department _SHIPPING_   Shift Assignment: A _____ B _X_ C _____

Work Unit _TRANSPORTATION_   Number Of Employees _6_

Union Affiliation _INTERNATIONAL SOCIETY OF TRUCK DRIVING_

Supervisor(s) _____   Phone No(s). _____

CHUCK FLEMMING   _000-0000_

Incumbent(s) _JIM BELL_   Badge/SSN _3353_

Job Description: Reviewed _X_   To Update _____   Not-Available _____

JOB SUMMARY

Reason the position exists (purpose):

The purpose of this position is to _TRANSPORT CARGO_

Production or Workload

PER CONTRACTED ASSIGNMENTS.

JOB FUNCTIONS

Essential Functions: Identify the critical duties actually performed by incumbents to fulfill the purpose of this position.

Write in prescribed sentence structure: action verb, object, [to] outcome, using M, E, T, W/A (machines, equipment, etc.).

Mark the "critical" box if not performing the duty would interrupt the flow of work. Include the daily % of time spent performing the critical duties. May not equal 100% due to performance of marginal duties.

DAILY % TIME	CRITICAL	ACTION VERB	OBJECT	[TO] OUTCOME/METW/A
10%	✔	Reads	Instructions	To complete the form
25%	✔	DRIVES	SEMI-TRACTOR TRAILERS	TO TRANSPORT OVERSIZED CARGO
40%	✔	DRIVES	TRUCKS	TO PICK UP AND DELIVER CARGO AT DESIGNATED LOCATIONS.
20%	✔	VERIFIES AND SECURES	CARGO	TO ENSURE SAFE TRANSPORT.
		LOADS	CARGO	TO EXPEDITE SHIPPING.
		PREPARES	MANIFESTS	TO IDENTIFY CONTENTS OF SHIPMENT.

ESSENTIAL FUNCTIONS CRITERIA CHECKLIST

POSITION TITLE: _TRUCK DRIVER_

FUNCTION: _DRIVES SEMI-TRACTOR TRAILERS TO TRANSPORT OVERSIZED LOADS._

(Complete a checklist for each function)

PRIMARY CONSIDERATIONS	YES	NO
1. Do incumbents actually perform the function?	☒	☐
2. Would removing the function fundamentally change the position?	☒	☐

REASONS TO CONSIDER	YES	NO
1. Does the position exist to perform the function?	☒	☐
2. Are there a limited number of employees who could perform the function?	☒	☐
3. Are the functions highly specialized?	☐	☒

EVIDENCE TO CONSIDER	YES	NO
1. Employers judgement that the function is essential?	☒	☐
2. Does a written Job Description include the function?	☒	☐
3. Is there a significant amount of time spent performing the function?	☒	☐
4. Are there serious consequences in not performing the function?	☒	☐
5. Is there a Collective Bargaining Agreement?	☒	☐

Function is Essential: ☒ ☐

Analyst Name _R. THRUSH_   Date _6-26-92_

Incumbent's Name _J. BELL_   Date _6-26-92_

Supervisor Name _C. FLEMMING_   Date _6-26-92_

ESSENTIAL FUNCTIONS CRITERIA CHECKLIST

POSITION TITLE: _TRUCK DRIVER_

FUNCTION: _LOADS CARGO TO EXPEDITE SHIPPING_

(Complete a checklist for each function)

PRIMARY CONSIDERATIONS	YES	NO
1. Do incumbents actually perform the function?	☒	☐
2. Would removing the function fundamentally change the position?	☐	☒

REASONS TO CONSIDER	YES	NO
1. Does the position exist to perform the function?	☐	☒
2. Are there a limited number of employees who could perform the function?	☐	☒
3. Are the functions highly specialized?	☐	☒

EVIDENCE TO CONSIDER	YES	NO
1. Employers judgement that the function is essential?	☐	☒
2. Does a written Job Description include the function?	☒	☐
3. Is there a significant amount of time spent performing the function?	☐	☒
4. Are there serious consequences in not performing the function?	☐	☒
5. Is there a Collective Bargaining Agreement?	☒	☐

Function is Essential: _(MARGINAL)_ ☐ ☒

Analyst Name _R. THRUSH_ Date _6-26-92_

Incumbent's Name _J. BELL_ Date _6-26-92_

Supervisor Name _C. FLEMMING_ Date _6-26-92_

ORGANIZATIONAL RELATIONSHIPS

Identify as specifically as possible the relationship of the assigned work unit to the department and to the organization as a whole. Briefly state the overall purpose of the work unit and/or department to the organization. Sketch an organizational flowchart of the relationship of the work unit and/or department to the nearest related work units or departments.

Identify as specifically as possible the specific names and titles of the people who report to this position, and the name and title who this position reports to.

```
                    ┌──────────────────┐
                    │    WAREHOUSE     │
                    │     MANAGER      │
                    └────────┬─────────┘
              ┌──────────────┴──────────────┐
    ┌─────────┴──────────┐       ┌──────────┴──────────┐
    │ SHIPPING DEPARTMENT│       │ RECEIVING DEPARTMENT│
    │      MANAGER       │       │       MANAGER       │
    └────┬───────────────┘       └─────────────────────┘
 ┌───────┴──────────┐
 │ TRANSPORTATION   │
 │   SUPERVISOR     │
 └───────┬──────────┘
 ┌───────┴──────────┐
 │    INCUMBENT     │
 └──────────────────┘
```

JOB REQUIREMENTS

PHYSICAL FACTORS

KEY:	NP	=	Not Present	O	=	1/3 of the day
	F	=	1/3–2/3 of the day	C	=	Over 2/3 of the day

FACTOR 1:   STRENGTH

MOBILITY   **FREQUENCY**

						NP	O	F	C
A.	Stand	_____ % of time	*2*	hrs/day		❏	☒	❏	❏
B.	Walk	_____ % of time	*2*	hrs/day		❏	☒	❏	❏
C.	Sit	_____ % of time	*4*	hrs/day		❏	❏	☒	❏
		___100%___	___4⑧10___ hrs/day						

COMMENTS: _SITS TO DRIVE TRUCKS AND AWAIT MOVEMENT OF LOADS_

_____

_____

LIFTING   **FREQUENCY**

	NP	O	F	C
up to 5 lbs	❏	❏	☒	❏
6 - 10 lbs	❏	❏	☒	❏
11 - 20 lbs	❏	❏	☒	❏
21 - 25 lbs	❏	☒	❏	❏
26 - 50 lbs	❏	☒	❏	❏
51 - 75 lbs	☒	❏	❏	❏
76 - 100 lbs	☒	❏	❏	❏
Over 100 lbs	☒	❏	❏	❏

COMMENTS: (Heaviest item and range of vertical distance) _____

LOAD AND TIE DOWN EQUIPMENT, TO READJUST LOAD, TO ASSIST TO

OFF LOAD CARGO.

_____

_____

_____

FACTOR 1: STRENGTH Continued

CARRYING

FREQUENCY

	NP	O	F	C
up to 5 lbs	☐	☒	☐	☐
6 - 10 lbs	☐	☒	☐	☐
11 - 20 lbs..	☐	☒	☐	☐
21 - 25 lbs	☐	☒	☐	☐
26 - 50 lbs	☒	☐	☐	☐
51 - 75 lbs	☒	☐	☐	☐
76 - 100 lbs	☒	☐	☐	☐
Over 100 lbs	☒	☐	☐	☐

COMMENTS: (Heaviest item and range of horizontal distance) *MINIMAL CARRYING REQUIRED DUE TO USE OF WAREHOUSE HANDLING EQUIPMENT AND WAREHOUSE WORKERS.*

PUSHING/PULLING

FREQUENCY

NOT MEASURED

	NP	O	F	C
5 lbs	☐	☐	☐	☐
6 - 10 lbs	☐	☐	☐	☐
11 - 20 lbs..	☐	☐	☐	☐
21 - 25 lbs	☐	☐	☐	☐
26 - 50 lbs	☐	☐	☐	☐
51 - 75 lbs	☐	☐	☐	☐
76 - 100 lbs	☐	☐	☐	☐.
Over 100 lbs	☐	☐	☐	☐

COMMENTS: (Wheeled objects, Footpedal, Lever, Equipment or Hand tool) *FREQUENT TO CONTINUOUS PUSHING UPON FOOT PEDALS TO DRIVE TRUCKS (PUSH STRENGTH VARIES WITH VEHICLE). OCCASIONALLY TO PUSH/PULL UPON TIED DOWN EQUIPMENT REQUIRING MAXIMUM STRENGTH.*

FACTOR 2: AGILITY

FREQUENCY

		NP	O	F	C
A.	Climbing...	☐	☒	☐	☐
B.	Balancing...	☐	☒	☐	☐
C.	Bending...	☐	☒	☐	☐
D.	Stooping...	☐	☒	☐	☐
E.	Crouching	☐	☒	☐	☐
F.	Kneeling...	☐	☒	☐	☐

FACTOR 2: AGILITY — Continued

FREQUENCY

		NP	O	F	C
G.	Crawling	☒	☐	☐	☐
H.	Running	☒	☐	☐	☐
I.	Twisting	☐	☒	☐	☐
J.	Turning	☐	☒	☐	☐
K.	Jumping	☒	☐	☐	☐

COMMENTS: _____

_____

_____

FACTOR 3: DEXTERITY

FREQUENCY

		NP	O	F	C
A.	Grasping–Firm/Strong	☐	☐	☐	☒
B.	Finger Dexterity	☐	☒	☐	☐
C.	Reaching Forward	☐	☐	☐	☒
D.	Reaching Overhead	☐	☒	☐	☐
E.	Pinching	☐	☒	☐	☐
F.	Grasping–Light	☒	☐	☐	☐

Dominant hand: ☒ Right ☐ Left ☐ Both

COMMENTS: _____

_____

_____

FACTOR 4: COORDINATION

FREQUENCY

		NP	O	F	C
A.	Eye - hand	☒	☐	☐	☐
B.	Eye - Hand - Foot	☐	☐	☒	☐
C.	Driving	☐	☐	☒	☐

COMMENTS: _____

_____

_____

FACTOR 5:   **VISION**

FREQUENCY

			NP	O	F	C
A.	Acuity, Near		☐	☐	☒	☐
B.	Acuity, Far		☐	☐	☒	☐
C.	Depth Perception		☐	☐	☒	☐
D.	Accommodation		☐	☐	☒	☐
E.	Color Vision		☒	☐	☐	☐
F.	Field of Vision		☐	☐	☒	☐

COMMENTS: _AS REQUIRED FOR TRUCK DRIVER CLASS DRIVERS LICENSE_

FACTOR 6:   **TALKING**

FREQUENCY

			NP	O	F	C
A.	Face-to-Face Contact		☐	☐	☒	☐
B.	Verbal Contact with Others		☐	☐	☒	☐
C.	Public		☒	☐	☐	☐

COMMENTS: _USES TELEPHONE AND TWO-WAY RADIO._

FACTOR 7:   **HEARING**

FREQUENCY

			NP	O	F	C
A.	Normal Conversation		☐	☐	☒	☐
B.	Telephone Communication		☐	☒	☐	☐
C.	Earplugs Required		☒	☐	☐	☐

COMMENTS: _'AS REQUIRED FOR TRUCK DRIVER CLASS DRIVERS LICENSE_

ENVIRONMENTAL FACTORS

FREQUENCY

		NP	O	F	C
A.	Works indoors	☐	☐	☒	☐
B.	Works outdoors	☐	☐	☒	☐
C.	Exposure to extreme hot or cold temperature	☒	☐	☐	☐
D.	Working at unprotected heights	☐	☒	☐	☐
E.	Being around moving machinery	☐	☒	☐	☐
F.	Exposure to marked changes in temperature/humidity	☒	☐	☐	☐
G.	Exposure to dust, fumes, smoke, gases, odors, mists or other irritating particles	☒	☐	☐	☐
	(specify) _____				
H.	Exposure to toxic or caustic chemicals	☒	☐	☐	☐
I.	Exposure to excessive noises	☐	☒	☐	☐
J.	Exposure to radiation or electrical energy	☒	☐	☐	☐
K.	Exposure to solvents, grease, or oils	☒	☐	☐	☐
L.	Exposure to slippery or uneven walking surfaces	☐	☒	☐	☐
M.	Working below ground	☒	☐	☐	☐
N.	Using computer (CRT) monitor	☒	☐	☐	☐
O.	Working with explosives	☒	☐	☐	☐
P.	Exposure to vibration	☐	☐	☒	☐
Q.	Exposure to flames or burning items	☒	☐	☐	☐
R.	Works around others	☐	☐	☒	☐
S.	Works alone	☐	☐	☒	☐
T.	Works with others	☐	☐	☒	☐

COMMENTS: (Describe special conditions) _OUTDOOR AREAS MAYBE OUTSIDE STORAGE AREAS OR OPEN WAREHOUSES._

SAFETY FACTORS

	PRESENT	NOT PRESENT
Material Safety Data Sheets		
(Verify Availability and Current)	☒	☐
Safety Equipment (Required to Wear)		
Safety Glasses	☐	☒
Ear Plugs	☐	☒
Hard Hat	☒	☐
Protective Clothing _GLOVES_	☒	☐
Other _RAIN GEAR-BOOTS, COAT, PANTS,_	☒	☐
_____	☐	☐

MACHINES • EQUIPMENT • TOOLS • WORK AIDS

MACHINES

Devices which are a combination of mechanical parts, power actuated and designed to apply force to do work on or move materials or to process data. Vehicles are considered to be machines.

LIST	SKILLED	OJT
18 SPEED DIESEL TRACTOR	☒	❏
CONTAINER, FLATBED, TANDOM TRAILERS	☒	❏
1/2 TON TO 1 1/2 HALF TON PICKUP TRUCKS	☒	❏
BOB TAIL TRUCKS	☒	❏
FORKLIFT	☒	❏
	❏	❏
	❏	❏
	❏	❏
	❏	❏
	❏	❏

EQUIPMENT

Devices which are power actuated and generally designed to be portable and used to apply a force to do work on or move material or to process data.

LIST	SKILLED	OJT
NONE	❏	❏
	❏	❏
	❏	❏
	❏	❏
	❏	❏
	❏	❏
	❏	❏
	❏	❏
	❏	❏
	❏	❏

MACHINES • EQUIPMENT • TOOLS • WORK AIDS

TOOLS

Devices or implements which are not power actuated and are manipulated by hand to do work on or move materials.

List	Skilled	OJT
TELEPHONE	☒	☐
TWO RAY RADIOS	☒	☐
HAND TRUCK	☒	☐
CARGO TIE DOWN DEVEICES	☒	☐
	☐	☐
	☐	☐
	☐	☐
	☐	☐
	☐	☐
	☐	☐

WORK AIDS

Items not considered to be a machine, equipment or tool yet are necessary for carrying out the work.

List	Skilled	OJT
NONE	☐	☐
	☐	☐
	☐	☐
	☐	☐
	☐	☐
	☐	☐
	☐	☐
	☐	☐
	☐	☐
	☐	☐

KEY

OJT–	The worker will need to learn to use upon commencing work in the position
Skilled–	The worker would need to have experience prior to commencing work in the position

JOB QUALIFICATIONS

MENTAL FACTORS

FACTOR 1   GENERAL EDUCATION DEVELOPMENT

REASONING

	PRESENT	NOT PRESENT
Deal with abstract and concrete variables, define problems, collect data, establish facts, and draw valid conclusions	❏	☒
Interpret instructions furnished in written, oral, diagrammatic, or schedule form	☒	❏
Deal with problems from standard situations	☒	❏
Carry out detailed but uninvolved written or oral instructions	☒	❏
Carry out single one or two step instructions	☒	❏

MATHEMATICS

	PRESENT	NOT PRESENT
COMPLEX SKILLS Business math, algebra, geometry, shopmath or statistics	☒	❏
SIMPLE SKILLS Add, subtract, multiply and divide whole numbers and fractions, make change, calculate time, calculate simple measurements	❏	❏

READING

	PRESENT	NOT PRESENT
COMPLEX SKILLS Comprehend newspapers, manuals, journals, instructions in use and maintenance of shop tools and equipment, safety rules and procedures and drawings	❏	☒
SIMPLE SKILLS English at the 6th grade level (tested), comprehend simple instructions or notations from a log book	☒	❏

ADA–Essential Function Identification

FACTOR 1	GENERAL EDUCATION DEVELOPMENT	continued

WRITING   **PRESENT**   **NOT PRESENT**

COMPLEX SKILLS

Prepare business letters, summaries of reports using
prescribed format and conforming to all rules of spelling,
punctuation, grammar, diction and style .... ❑   ☒

SIMPLE SKILLS

English sentences containing subject, verb and object;
names and addresses, complete job application or
notations in a log book .... ☒   ❑

FACTOR 2	EDUCATIONAL ACHIEVEMENT

High School: ☒ Yes   ❑ No

College Degree: ❑ Associate   ❑ Bachelor   ❑ Masters   ❑ Doctorate

Trade School: (Specify) _____

_____

_____

_____

_____

_____

FACTOR 3	EXPERIENCE/KNOWLEDGE DESIRED

(Specify type and duration) _A MINIMUM OF FIVE YEARS DRIVING TRACTOR-TRAILERS AND_
TRUCKS TO TRANSPORT CARGO ON HIGHWAYS. KNOWLEDGE OF DEPARTMENT OF
TRANSPORTATION CARGO TRANSPORT RULES, REGULATIONS AND POLICIES.

_____

_____

_____

FACTOR 4	LICENSE/CERTIFICATION

Valid Drivers License: ☒ Yes   ❑ No

Other: (Specify) _POSSESS VALID TRUCK DRIVERS LICENSE WITH CURRENT HEALTH CARD_
HAVE NO INFRACTIONS ON DRIVING RECORD FOR THREE YEARS
ABILITY TO OBTAIN TOP SECRET SECURITY CLEARANCE.

_____

_____

FACTOR 5 — PERCEPTION

	PRESENT	NOT PRESENT
SPATIAL:	☒	☐

Ability to comprehend forms in space and understand relationships of plane and solid objects. May be used in such tasks as blueprint reading and in solving geometry problems. Frequently described as the ability to "visualize" objects of two or three dimensions, or to think visually of geometric forms.

	PRESENT	NOT PRESENT
FORM:	☐	☒

Ability to perceive pertinent detail in objects or in pictorial or graphic material. To make visual comparisons and discriminations and see slight differences in shapes and shadings of figures and widths and lengths of line.

	PRESENT	NOT PRESENT
CLERICAL:	☐	☒

Ability to perceive pertinent detail in verbal or tabular material. To observe differences in copy, to proof-read words and numbers, and to avoid perceptual errors in arithmetic computation.

FACTOR 6 — DATA

Information, knowledge, and conceptions, related to data, people, or things, obtained by observation, and mental creation. Data are intangible and include numbers, words, symbols, ideas, concepts, and oral verbalization.

	PRESENT	NOT PRESENT
SYNTHESIZING	☐	☒
COORDINATING	☐	☒
ANALYZING	☐	☒
COMPILING	☐	☒
COMPUTING	☐	☒
COPYING	☐	☒
COMPARING.	☒	☐

FACTOR 7	PEOPLE

Human beings; also animals dealt with on an individual basis as if they were human.

	PRESENT	NOT PRESENT
MENTORING	☐	☒
NEGOTIATING	☐	☒
INSTRUCTION	☐	☒
SUPERVISING	☐	☒
DIVERTING	☐	☒
PERSUADING	☐	☒
SPEAKING-SIGNALING	☒	☐
SERVING	☐	☒
TAKING INSTRUCTIONS-HELPING	☒	☐

FACTOR 8	THINGS

Inanimate objects as distinguished from human beings, substances, or materials; machines, tools, equipment and products. A thing is tangible and has shape, form, and other physical characteristics.

	PRESENT	NOT PRESENT
SETTING UP	☐	☒
PRECISION WORKING	☐	☒
OPERATING-CONTROLLING	☐	☒
DRIVING-OPERATION	☒	☐
MANIPULATING	☐	☒
TENDING	☐	☒
FEEDING-OFFBEARING	☐	☒
HANDLING	☒	☐

FACTOR 9	PERSONAL TRAITS

Work functions required by specific job-worker situations.

	PRESENT	NOT PRESENT

I. ABILITY TO COMPREHEND AND FOLLOW INSTRUCTIONS .... ☒ ☐

The ability to maintain attention and concentration for necessary periods; to apply common sense understanding to carry out instructions furnished in written, oral or diagrammatic form; to adapt to situations requiring the precise attainment of set limits, tolerances or standards; to operate–controls which involve starting, stopping, controlling and adjusting the progress of a machine or piece of equipment.

II. ABILITY TO PERFORM SIMPLE AND REPETITIVE TASKS .... ☒ ☐

The ability to ask simple questions or request assistance; to perform activities of a routine, concrete, organized nature; to remember locations and work procedures; to make decisions based on simple sensory data.

III. ABILITY TO MAINTAIN A WORK PACE APPROPRIATE TO A GIVEN WORK LOAD .... ☒ ☐

The ability to perform activities with a schedule, maintain regular attendance and to be punctual within specified tolerances; to complete a normal work day and/or work week and perform at a consistent pace without unreasonable number and/or length of rest periods; to perform effectively when confronted with potential emergency, critical, unusual or dangerous situations, or in situations in which working speed and sustained attention are make or break aspects of the job (i.e., police work, fire fighter, life guard, crossing guard, security guard, bouncer, body guard, paramedic, emergency room personnel, ICU/CCU nurse, etc.

IV. ABILITY TO RELATE TO OTHER PEOPLE BEYOND GIVING AND RECEIVING INSTRUCTIONS .... ☐ ☒

The ability to get along with co–workers or peers without exhibiting extreme responses; to perform work activities requiring negotiating with, instructing, supervising, persuading or speaking; to respond appropriately to criticism from a supervisor.

V. ABILITY TO INFLUENCE PEOPLE .... ☐ ☒

The ability to convince or redirect others; to understand the meanings of words and to use them effectively; to interact appropriately with the general public.

VI. ABILITY TO PERFORM COMPLEX OR VARIED TASKS .... ☐ ☒

The ability to synthesize, coordinate and analyze data; to perform jobs requiring precise attainment of set limits, tolerances or standards.

VII. ABILITY TO MAKE GENERALIZATIONS, EVALUATIONS OR DECISIONS WITHOUT IMMEDIATE SUPERVISION .... ☐ ☒

The ability to retain awareness of potential hazards and observe appropriate precautions; to understand and remember detailed instructions; to travel in unfamiliar places or use public transportation systems.

VIII. ABILITY TO ACCEPT AND CARRY OUT RESPONSIBILITY FOR DIRECTION, CONTROL AND PLANNING .... ☐ ☒

The ability to set realistic goals or make plans independently of others; to negotiate with, instruct or supervise people; to respond appropriately to changes in the work setting.

Essential Functions–Demands Job Analysis Worksheet

Date _1-27-93_   Job Analyst _R. THRUSH_

JOB INFORMATION

Title _CUSTODIAN I_   Employer _AZTEC TOWERS_

Job Code _664_   Labor Grade _2_   Salary/Rate _$1450 PER MONTH_

Department _OPERATIONS_   Shift Assignment: A _____   B _____   C _X_

Work Unit _CUSTODIAL_   Number Of Employees _12_

Union Affiliation _NONE_

Supervisor(s) _____   Phone No(s). _____

   MIKE PITTS   _000-0000_

Incumbent(s) _JANICE SCOTT_   Badge/SSN _44185_

   BARRY HANES   _44161_

Job Description: Reviewed _X_   To Update _____   Not-Available _____

JOB SUMMARY

Reason the position exists (purpose):

The purpose of this position is to _ENSURE ASSIGNED AREAS ARE CLEAN, SECURE,_

ORDERLY AND SAFE.

Production or Workload

REQUIRED TO DUST AND EMPTY TRASH ON ENTIRE FLOOR ASSIGNED NIGHTLEY

VACUUM ONE-HALF FLOOR AREA NIGHTLY; CLEAN ONE OF THREE SETS OF

BATHROOMS NIGHTLY; REPLENISH PAPER AND EMPTY TRASH IN ALL BATHROOMS

NIGHTLY. ASSIST TO CLEAN ADDITIONAL FLOORS AS ASSIGNED NIGHTLY.

JOB FUNCTIONS

Essential Functions: Identify the critical duties actually performed by incumbents to fulfill the purpose of this position.

Write in prescribed sentence structure: action verb, object, [to] outcome, using M, E, T, W/A (machines, equipment, etc.).

Mark the "critical" box if not performing the duty would interrupt the flow of work. Include the daily % of time spent performing the critical duties. May not equal 100% due to performance of marginal duties.

DAILY % TIME	CRITICAL	ACTION VERB	OBJECT	[TO] OUTCOME/METW/A
10%	✔	*Reads*	*Instructions*	*To complete the form*
50%	✔	CLEANS	FLOORS, WALLS	TO REMOVE DIRT, DEBRIS AND SPILLS USING RAGS, BROOMS, MOPS,
			CARPETS FURNITURE	VACUUM, SHAMPOOER, BUFFERS AND CLEANING AGENTS.
			AND WALKWAYS	
30%	✔	DISINFECTS	BATHROOMS, SHOWERS,	TO REMOVE AND INHIBIT THE GROWTH OF BACTERIA AND GERMS USING RAGS,
			AND PUBLIC AREAS	BRUSHES, BROOMS, MOPS, GLOVES AND CLEANING AGENTS.
5%	✔	INSPECTS	DOORS, WINDOWS,	TO SAFEGUARD DISTRICT PROPERTY USING KEYS, LOCKS AND FLASHLIGHT.
			LOCKS, LIGHTS AND EQUIPMENT	
5%	✔	ARRANGES	FURNITURE AND EQUIPMENT	TO ORGANIZE ROOMS FOR EVENTS AND MEETINGS USING CARTS,
				DOLLIES AND ELECTRIC CART.
5%	✔	REPLENISHES	PAPER, LIQUID AND POWDER	TO ASSURE ADEQUATE SUPPLY ON HAND USING SMALL HAND TOOLS
			DISPENSERS	KEYS AND FUNNEL.
1%	✔	REPORTS	SANITARY AND SAFETY	TO ENHANCE THE HEALTH AND SAFETY OF STUDENTS, STAFF, AND THE
			HAZARDS, VANDALISM,	PUBLIC USING TELEPHONE, SIGNS, FORMS, TAGS AND WRITING UTENSILS.
			AND UNAUTHORIZED	
			PERSONNEL	

ESSENTIAL FUNCTIONS CRITERIA CHECKLIST

POSITION TITLE: _CUSTODIAN I_

FUNCTION: _CLEANS FLOORS, CARPETS, WALLS, FURNITURE AND WALKWAYS._
TO REMOVE DIRT, DEBRIS AND SPILLS USING RAGS, BROOMS,
MOPS, VACUUM CLEANER AND CLEANING AGENTS.

(Complete a checklist for each function)

PRIMARY CONSIDERATIONS	**YES**	**No**
1. Do incumbents actually perform the function?	☒	☐
2. Would removing the function fundamentally change the position?	☒	☐

REASONS TO CONSIDER	**YES**	**No**
1. Does the position exist to perform the function?	☒	☐
2. Are there a limited number of employees who could perform the function?	☒	☐
3. Are the functions highly specialized?	☐	☒

EVIDENCE TO CONSIDER	**YES**	**No**
1. Employers judgement that the function is essential?	☒	☐
2. Does a written Job Description include the function?	☒	☐
3. Is there a significant amount of time spent performing the function?	☒	☐
4. Are there serious consequences in not performing the function?	☒	☐
5. Is there a Collective Bargaining Agreement?	☐	☒

Function is Essential:	☒	☐

Analyst Name _____R. THRUSH_____ Date ___1-27-93___

Incumbent's Name _J. SCOTT, B. HANKS_ Date ___1-27-93___

Supervisor Name __M. PITTS__ Date ___1-27-93___

ESSENTIAL FUNCTIONS CRITERIA CHECKLIST

POSITION TITLE: _CUSTODIAN I_

FUNCTION: _DISINFECTS BATHROOMS, SHOWERS, AND PUBLIC AREAS. TO REMOVE AND INHIBIT THE GROWTH OF BACTERIA AND GERMS USING RAGS, BRUSHES, BROOMS, MOPS, GLOVES AND CLEANING AGENTS._

(Complete a checklist for each function)

PRIMARY CONSIDERATIONS	YES	NO
1. Do incumbents actually perform the function?	☒	☐
2. Would removing the function fundamentally change the position?	☒	☐

REASONS TO CONSIDER	YES	NO
1. Does the position exist to perform the function?	☒	☐
2. Are there a limited number of employees who could perform the function?	☒	☐
3. Are the functions highly specialized?	☐	☒

EVIDENCE TO CONSIDER	YES	NO
1. Employers judgement that the function is essential?	☒	☐
2. Does a written Job Description include the function?	☒	☐
3. Is there a significant amount of time spent performing the function?	☒	☐
4. Are there serious consequences in not performing the function?	☒	☐
5. Is there a Collective Bargaining Agreement?	☐	☒

Function is Essential:	☒	☐

Analyst Name _R. THRUSH_   Date _1-27-93_

Incumbent's Name _J. SCOTT, B. HANKS_   Date _1-27-93_

Supervisor Name _M. PITTS_   Date _1-27-93_

ESSENTIAL FUNCTIONS CRITERIA CHECKLIST

POSITION TITLE: _CUSTODIAN I_

FUNCTION: _INSPECTS DOORS, WINDOWS, LOCKS, LIGHTS AND EQUIPMENT._
TO SAFEGUARD PROPERTY USING KEYS, LOCKS, AND
FLASHLIGHT.

(Complete a checklist for each function)

PRIMARY CONSIDERATIONS	YES	NO
1. Do incumbents actually perform the function?	☒	☐
2. Would removing the function fundamentally change the position?	☒	☐

REASONS TO CONSIDER	YES	NO
1. Does the position exist to perform the function?	☒	☐
2. Are there a limited number of employees who could perform the function?	☒	☐
3. Are the functions highly specialized?	☐	☒

EVIDENCE TO CONSIDER	YES	NO
1. Employers judgement that the function is essential?	☒	☐
2. Does a written Job Description include the function?	☒	☐
3. Is there a significant amount of time spent performing the function?	☒	☐
4. Are there serious consequences in not performing the function?	☒	☐
5. Is there a Collective Bargaining Agreement?	☐	☒

Function is Essential:	☒	☐

Analyst Name ___R. THRUSH___ Date ___1-27-93___

Incumbent's Name ___J. SCOTT, B. HANKS___ Date ___1-27-93___

Supervisor Name ___M. PITTS___ Date ___1-27-93___

ESSENTIAL FUNCTIONS CRITERIA CHECKLIST

POSITION TITLE: _CUSTODIAN I_

FUNCTION: _ARRANGES FURNITURE AND EQUIPMENT. TO ORGANIZE ROOMS FOR EVENTS AND MEETINGS USING CARTS, DOLLIES AND ELECTRIC CART._

(Complete a checklist for each function)

PRIMARY CONSIDERATIONS	YES	NO
1. Do incumbents actually perform the function?	☒	☐
2. Would removing the function fundamentally change the position?	☒	☐

REASONS TO CONSIDER	YES	NO
1. Does the position exist to perform the function?	☒	☐
2. Are there a limited number of employees who could perform the function?	☒	☐
3. Are the functions highly specialized?	☐	☒

EVIDENCE TO CONSIDER	YES	NO
1. Employers judgement that the function is essential?	☒	☐
2. Does a written Job Description include the function?	☒	☐
3. Is there a significant amount of time spent performing the function?	☒	☐
4. Are there serious consequences in not performing the function?	☒	☐
5. Is there a Collective Bargaining Agreement?	☐	☒

Function is Essential: ☒ ☐

Analyst Name _____R. THRUSH_____ Date __1-27-93__

Incumbent's Name __J. SCOTT, B. HANKS__ Date __1-27-93__

Supervisor Name __M. PITTS__ Date __1-27-93__

ESSENTIAL FUNCTIONS CRITERIA CHECKLIST

POSITION TITLE: _CUSTODIAN I_

FUNCTION: _REPLENISHES PAPER, POWDER AND LIQUID DISPENSERS, TO ASSURE ADEQUATE SUPPLY ON HAND USING SMALL HAND TOOLS, KEYS AND FUNNEL._

(Complete a checklist for each function)

PRIMARY CONSIDERATIONS	YES	NO
1. Do incumbents actually perform the function?	☒	☐
2. Would removing the function fundamentally change the position?	☒	☐

REASONS TO CONSIDER	YES	NO
1. Does the position exist to perform the function?	☒	☐
2. Are there a limited number of employees who could perform the function?	☒	☐
3. Are the functions highly specialized?	☐	☒

EVIDENCE TO CONSIDER	YES	NO
1. Employers judgement that the function is essential?	☒	☐
2. Does a written Job Description include the function?	☒	☐
3. Is there a significant amount of time spent performing the function?	☒	☐
4. Are there serious consequences in not performing the function?	☒	☐
5. Is there a Collective Bargaining Agreement?	☐	☒

	YES	NO
Function is Essential:	☒	☐

Analyst Name _R. THRUSH_ Date _1-27-93_

Incumbent's Name _J. SCOTT, B. HANKS_ Date _1-27-93_

Supervisor Name _M. PITTS_ Date _1-27-93_

ESSENTIAL FUNCTIONS CRITERIA CHECKLIST

POSITION TITLE: _CUSTODIAN I_

FUNCTION: _REPORTS SANITARY AND SAFETY HAZARDS, VANDALISM, AND UNAUTHORIZED PERSONNEL TO ENHANCE THE HEALTH AND SAFETY OF STUDENTS, STAFF AND THE PUBLIC USING TELEPHONE, SIGNS, FORMS, TAGS AND WRITING UTENSILS._

(Complete a checklist for each function)

PRIMARY CONSIDERATIONS	YES	NO
1. Do incumbents actually perform the function?	☒	☐
2. Would removing the function fundamentally change the position?	☒	☐

REASONS TO CONSIDER	YES	NO
1. Does the position exist to perform the function?	☒	☐
2. Are there a limited number of employees who could perform the function?	☒	☐
3. Are the functions highly specialized?	☐	☒

EVIDENCE TO CONSIDER	YES	NO
1. Employers judgement that the function is essential?	☒	☐
2. Does a written Job Description include the function?	☒	☐
3. Is there a significant amount of time spent performing the function?	☒	☐
4. Are there serious consequences in not performing the function?	☒	☐
5. Is there a Collective Bargaining Agreement?	☐	☒

	YES	NO
Function is Essential:	☒	☐

Analyst Name _R. THRUSH_   Date _1-27-93_

Incumbent's Name _J. SCOTT, B. HANKS_   Date _1-27-93_

Supervisor Name _M. PITTS_   Date _1-27-93_

ORGANIZATIONAL RELATIONSHIPS

Identify as specifically as possible the relationship of the assigned work unit to the department and to the organization as a whole. Briefly state the overall purpose of the work unit and/or department to the organization. Sketch an organizational flowchart of the relationship of the work unit and/or department to the nearest related work units or departments.

Identify as specifically as possible the specific names and titles of the people who report to this position, and the name and title who this position reports to.

```
                    ┌──────────────────────┐
                    │ BUILDING MAINTENANCE │
                    │      MANAGER         │
                    └──────────────────────┘
          ┌───────────────┼───────────────┐
┌───────────────┐ ┌───────────────┐ ┌───────────────┐
│CUSTODIAL FOREMAN│ │CUSTODIAL FOREMAN│ │CUSTODIAL FOREMAN│
│    C SHIFT    │ │    B SHIFT    │ │    A SHIFT    │
└───────────────┘ └───────────────┘ └───────────────┘
          │
┌───────────────┐
│   INCUMBENT   │
└───────────────┘
```

JOB REQUIREMENTS

PHYSICAL FACTORS

KEY:	NP	=	Not Present	O	=	1/3 of the day
	F	=	1/3–2/3 of the day	C	=	Over 2/3 of the day

FACTOR 1: STRENGTH

MOBILITY   FREQUENCY

				NP	O	F	C
A.	Stand _15_ % of time _____ hrs/day			❑	☒	❑	❑
B.	Walk _80_ % of time _____ hrs/day			❑	❑	❑	☒
C.	Sit _5_ % of time _____ hrs/day			❑	☒	❑	❑

_100%_   _4/8/10_ hrs/day

COMMENTS: _____

_____

_____

LIFTING   FREQUENCY

	NP	O	F	C
up to 5 lbs	❑	❑	❑	☒
6 - 10 lbs	❑	❑	❑	☒
11 - 20 lbs	❑	❑	☒	❑
21 - 25 lbs	❑	☒	❑	❑
26 - 50 lbs	❑	☒	❑	❑
51 - 75 lbs	☒	❑	❑	❑
76 - 100 lbs	☒	❑	❑	❑
Over 100 lbs	☒	❑	❑	❑

COMMENTS: (Heaviest item and range of vertical distance) _ON A WEEKLY TO MONTHLY BASIS LIFTS AT WAIST HEIGHT, A CASE OF PAPER PRODUCTS TO REPLENISH SUPPLY IN STORAGE CLOSET ON ASSIGNED FLOOR._

_____

_____

_____

FACTOR 1:   STRENGTH   Continued

CARRYING   FREQUENCY

	NP	O	F	C
up to 5 lbs	☐	☐	☒	☐
6 - 10 lbs	☐	☐	☒	☐
11 - 20 lbs	☐	☐	☒	☐
21 - 25 lbs	☐	☒	☐	☐
26 - 50 lbs	☐	☒	☐	☐
51 - 75 lbs	☒	☐	☐	☐
76 - 100 lbs	☒	☐	☐	☐
Over 100 lbs	☒	☐	☐	☐

COMMENTS: (Heaviest item and range of horizontal distance) _TO ASSIST TO MOVE A DESK OR CHAIR IN AN OFFICE AREA OF LESS THAN 25 FEET._

PUSHING/PULLING   FREQUENCY

	NP	O	F	C
5 lbs	☐	☐	☐	☒
6 - 10 lbs	☐	☐	☒	☐
11 - 20 lbs	☐	☐	☒	☐
21 - 25 lbs	☐	☐	☒	☐
26 - 50 lbs	☐	☐	☒	☐
51 - 75 lbs	☒	☐	☐	☐
76 - 100 lbs	☒	☐	☐	☐.
Over 100 lbs	☒	☐	☐	☐

COMMENTS: (Wheeled objects, Footpedal, Lever, Equipment or Hand tool) _NIGHTLY TO PUSH WHEELED TRASH RECEPTACLE, WHEELED MOP BUCKET, TO USE BROOM, MOP, VACUUM CLEANER AND RAGS._

FACTOR 2:   AGILITY

         FREQUENCY

		NP	O	F	C
A.	Climbing	☐	☒	☐	☐
B.	Balancing	☐	☒	☐	☐
C.	Bending	☐	☒	☐	☐
D.	Stooping	☐	☒	☐	☐
E.	Crouching	☐	☒	☐	☐
F.	Kneeling	☐	☒	☐	☐

FACTOR 2: AGILITY — Continued

FREQUENCY

			NP	O	F	C
G.	Crawling		☒	☐	☐	☐
H.	Running		☒	☐	☐	☐
I.	Twisting		☐	☒	☐	☐
J.	Turning		☐	☒	☐	☐
K.	Jumping		☒	☐	☐	☐

COMMENTS: _____

_____

_____

FACTOR 3: DEXTERITY

FREQUENCY

			NP	O	F	C
A.	Grasping–Firm/Strong		☐	☐	☐	☒
B.	Finger Dexterity		☐	☒	☐	☐
C.	Reaching Forward		☐	☐	☐	☒
D.	Reaching Overhead		☐	☒	☐	☐
E.	Pinching		☐	☒	☐	☐
F.	Grasping–Light		☒	☐	☐	☐

Dominant hand: ☒ Right ☐ Left ☐ Both

COMMENTS: _____

_____

_____

FACTOR 4: COORDINATION

FREQUENCY

			NP	O	F	C
A.	Eye - hand		☐	☐	☐	☒
B.	Eye - Hand - Foot		☒	☐	☐	☐
C.	Driving		☒	☐	☐	☐

COMMENTS: _____

_____

_____

FACTOR 5: VISION

FREQUENCY

		NP	O	F	C
A.	Acuity, Near	❏	❏	❏	☒
B.	Acuity, Far	❏	❏	❏	☒
C.	Depth Perception	☒	❏	❏	❏
D.	Accommodation	☒	❏	❏	❏
E.	Color Vision	☒	❏	❏	❏
F.	Field of Vision	☒	❏	❏	❏

COMMENTS: _____

_____

_____

FACTOR 6: TALKING

FREQUENCY

		NP	O	F	C
A.	Face-to-Face Contact	❏	☒	❏	❏
B.	Verbal Contact with Others	☒	❏	❏	❏
C.	Public	☒	❏	❏	❏

COMMENTS: _____

_____

_____

FACTOR 7: HEARING

FREQUENCY

		NP	O	F	C
A.	Normal Conversation	❏	☒	❏	❏
B.	Telephone Communication	☒	❏	❏	❏
C.	Earplugs Required	☒	❏	❏	❏

COMMENTS: _____

_____

_____

ENVIRONMENTAL FACTORS

		FREQUENCY			
		NP	**O**	**F**	**C**
A.	Works indoors	❑	❑	❑	☒
B.	Works outdoors	☒	❑	❑	❑
C.	Exposure to extreme hot or cold temperature	☒	❑	❑	❑
D.	Working at unprotected heights	☒	❑	❑	❑
E.	Being around moving machinery	☒	❑	❑	❑
F.	Exposure to marked changes in temperature/humidity	☒	❑	❑	❑
G.	Exposure to dust, fumes, smoke, gases, odors, mists or other irritating particles	❑	❑	☒	❑
	(specify) *CLEANING DUST, CLEANING SOLUTION FUMES*				
H.	Exposure to toxic or caustic chemicals	☒	❑	❑	❑
I.	Exposure to excessive noises	☒	❑	❑	❑
J.	Exposure to radiation or electrical energy	☒	❑	❑	❑
K.	Exposure to solvents, grease, or oils	☒	❑	❑	❑
L.	Exposure to slippery or uneven walking surfaces	❑	☒	❑	❑
M.	Working below ground	☒	❑	❑	❑
N.	Using computer (CRT) monitor	☒	❑	❑	❑
O.	Working with explosives	☒	❑	❑	❑
P.	Exposure to vibration	☒	❑	❑	❑
Q.	Exposure to flames or burning items	☒	❑	❑	❑
R.	Works around others	☒	❑	❑	❑
S.	Works alone	❑	❑	❑	☒
T.	Works with others	❑	☒	❑	❑

COMMENTS: (Describe special conditions) _____

_____

_____

SAFETY FACTORS

	PRESENT	**NOT PRESENT**
Material Safety Data Sheets		
(Verify Availability and Current)	☒	❑
Safety Equipment (Required to Wear)		
Safety Glasses	❑	☒
Ear Plugs	❑	☒
Hard Hat	❑	☒
Protective Clothing .... *RUBBER GLOVES*	☒	❑
Other _____	❑	❑
_____	❑	❑

MACHINES • EQUIPMENT • TOOLS • WORK AIDS

MACHINES

Devices which are a combination of mechanical parts, power actuated and designed to apply force to do work on or move materials or to process data. Vehicles are considered to be machines.

LIST	SKILLED	OJT
NONE	❑	❑
	❑	❑
	❑	❑
	❑	❑
	❑	❑
	❑	❑
	❑	❑
	❑	❑
	❑	❑
	❑	❑

EQUIPMENT

Devices which are power actuated and generally designed to be portable and used to apply a force to do work on or move material or to process data.

LIST	SKILLED	OJT
VACUUM CLEANER	☒	❑
BUFFER	☒	❑
CARPET STEAM CLEANER	❑	☒
SHAMPOOER	❑	☒
	❑	❑
	❑	❑
	❑	❑
	❑	❑
	❑	❑
	❑	❑

MACHINES • EQUIPMENT • TOOLS • WORK AIDS

TOOLS

Devices or implements which are not power actuated and are manipulated by hand to do work on or move materials.

LIST	SKILLED	OJT
MOPS, BROOMS, BRUSHES, RAGS	☒	☐
MOP BUCKET WITH WRINGER	☒	☐
3 FOOT STEP LADDER	☒	☐
SPRAY BOTTLES	☒	☐
2-WHEEL DOLLY	☒	☐
WHEELED TRASH BIN	☒	☐
DUSTER	☒	☐
HAND TOOLS	☒	☐
	☐	☐
	☐	☐

WORK AIDS

Items not considered to be a machine, equipment or tool yet are necessary for carrying out the work.

LIST	SKILLED	OJT
RUBBER GLOVES	☒	☐
SPONGES	☒	☐
PAPER TOWELS	☒	☐
KEYS	☒	☐
FLASHLIGHT	☒	☐
CLEANING SOLUTIONS	☒	☐
SIGNS, TAGS, WRITING UTENSILS	☒	☐
TELEPHONE	☒	☐
	☐	☐
	☐	☐

KEY

OJT– The worker will need to learn to use upon commencing work in the position

SKILLED– The worker would need to have experience prior to commencing work in the position

JOB QUALIFICATIONS

MENTAL FACTORS

FACTOR 1   GENERAL EDUCATION DEVELOPMENT

REASONING   PRESENT   NOT PRESENT

Deal with abstract and concrete variables, define problems,
collect data, establish facts, and draw valid conclusions .... ❏   ☒
Interpret instructions furnished in written, oral, diagrammatic,
or schedule form... ❏   ☒
Deal with problems from standard situations .... ❏   ☒
Carry out detailed but uninvolved written or oral instructions............. ❏   ☒
Carry out single one or two step instructions .... ☒   ❏

MATHEMATICS   PRESENT   NOT PRESENT

COMPLEX SKILLS
Business math, algebra, geometry,
shopmath or statistics... ❏   ☒

SIMPLE SKILLS
Add, subtract, multiply and divide whole numbers and
fractions, make change, calculate time, calculate
simple measurements .... ☒   ❏

READING   PRESENT   NOT PRESENT

COMPLEX SKILLS
Comprehend newspapers, manuals, journals, instructions
in use and maintenance of shop tools and equipment,
safety rules and procedures and drawings.. ❏   ☒

SIMPLE SKILLS
English at the 6th grade level (tested), comprehend
simple instructions or notations from a log book .... ☒   ❏

FACTOR 1	GENERAL EDUCATION DEVELOPMENT	continued

WRITING PRESENT NOT PRESENT

COMPLEX SKILLS

Prepare business letters, summaries of reports using
prescribed format and conforming to all rules of spelling,
punctuation, grammar, diction and style .... ☐ ☒

SIMPLE SKILLS

English sentences containing subject, verb and object;
names and addresses, complete job application or
notations in a log book .... ☒ ☐

FACTOR 2	EDUCATIONAL ACHIEVEMENT

High School: ☒ Yes ☐ No

College Degree: ☐ Associate ☐ Bachelor ☐ Masters ☐ Doctorate

Trade School: (Specify) _____

_____

_____

_____

_____

_____

FACTOR 3	EXPERIENCE/KNOWLEDGE DESIRED

(Specify type and duration) _SIX MONTHS EXPERIENCE GENERAL CLEANING AND KNOWLEDGE OF
STANDARD CLEANING PROCEDURES AND USE OF STANDARD CLEANING AGENTS. ABILITY
TO DEMONSTRATE KNOWLEDGE AND EXPERIENCE OF CUSTODIAL ACTIVITIES._

_____

_____

_____

FACTOR 4	LICENSE/CERTIFICATION

Valid Drivers License: ☒ Yes ☐ No

Other: (Specify) _____

_____

_____

_____

_____

FACTOR 5 — PERCEPTION

	PRESENT	NOT PRESENT
SPATIAL:	☐	☒

Ability to comprehend forms in space and understand relationships of plane and solid objects. May be used in such tasks as blueprint reading and in solving geometry problems. Frequently described as the ability to "visualize" objects of two or three dimensions, or to think visually of geometric forms.

	PRESENT	NOT PRESENT
FORM:	☐	☒

Ability to perceive pertinent detail in objects or in pictorial or graphic material. To make visual comparisons and discriminations and see slight differences in shapes and shadings of figures and widths and lengths of line.

	PRESENT	NOT PRESENT
CLERICAL:	☐	☒

Ability to perceive pertinent detail in verbal or tabular material. To observe differences in copy, to proof-read words and numbers, and to avoid perceptual errors in arithmetic computation.

FACTOR 6 — DATA

Information, knowledge, and conceptions, related to data, people, or things, obtained by observation, and mental creation. Data are intangible and include numbers, words, symbols, ideas, concepts, and oral verbalization.

	PRESENT	NOT PRESENT
SYNTHESIZING	☐	☒
COORDINATING	☐	☒
ANALYZING	☐	☒
COMPILING	☐	☒
COMPUTING	☒	☐
COPYING	☐	☒
COMPARING.	☐	☒

FACTOR 7	PEOPLE

Human beings; also animals dealt with on an individual basis as if they were human.

	PRESENT	NOT PRESENT
MENTORING	☐	☒
NEGOTIATING	☐	☒
INSTRUCTION	☐	☒
SUPERVISING	☐	☒
DIVERTING	☐	☒
PERSUADING	☐	☒
SPEAKING-SIGNALING	☐	☒
SERVING	☐	☒
TAKING INSTRUCTIONS-HELPING	☒	☐

FACTOR 8	THINGS

Inanimate objects as distinguished from human beings, substances, or materials; machines, tools, equipment and products. A thing is tangible and has shape, form, and other physical characteristics.

	PRESENT	NOT PRESENT
SETTING UP	☐	☒
PRECISION WORKING	☐	☒
OPERATING-CONTROLLING	☐	☒
DRIVING-OPERATION	☐	☒
MANIPULATING	☐	☒
TENDING	☐	☒
FEEDING-OFFBEARING	☐	☒
HANDLING	☒	☐

FACTOR 9 — PERSONAL TRAITS

Work functions required by specific job-worker situations.

	PRESENT	NOT PRESENT

I. ABILITY TO COMPREHEND AND FOLLOW INSTRUCTIONS .... ☒ ☐

The ability to maintain attention and concentration for necessary periods; to apply common sense understanding to carry out instructions furnished in written, oral or diagrammatic form; to adapt to situations requiring the precise attainment of set limits, tolerances or standards; to operate–controls which involve starting, stopping, controlling and adjusting the progress of a machine or piece of equipment.

II. ABILITY TO PERFORM SIMPLE AND REPETITIVE TASKS .... ☒ ☐

The ability to ask simple questions or request assistance; to perform activities of a routine, concrete, organized nature; to remember locations and work procedures; to make decisions based on simple sensory data.

III. ABILITY TO MAINTAIN A WORK PACE APPROPRIATE TO A GIVEN WORK LOAD .... ☒ ☐

The ability to perform activities with a schedule, maintain regular attendance and to be punctual within specified tolerances; to complete a normal work day and/or work week and perform at a consistent pace without unreasonable number and/or length of rest periods; to perform effectively when confronted with potential emergency, critical, unusual or dangerous situations, or in situations in which working speed and sustained attention are make or break aspects of the job (i.e., police work, fire fighter, life guard, crossing guard, security guard, bouncer, body guard, paramedic, emergency room personnel, ICU/CCU nurse, etc.).

IV. ABILITY TO RELATE TO OTHER PEOPLE BEYOND GIVING AND RECEIVING INSTRUCTIONS .... ☐ ☒

The ability to get along with co–workers or peers without exhibiting extreme responses; to perform work activities requiring negotiating with, instructing, supervising, persuading or speaking; to respond appropriately to criticism from a supervisor.

V. ABILITY TO INFLUENCE PEOPLE .... ☐ ☒

The ability to convince or redirect others; to understand the meanings of words and to use them effectively; to interact appropriately with the general public.

VI. ABILITY TO PERFORM COMPLEX OR VARIED TASKS .... ☐ ☒

The ability to synthesize, coordinate and analyze data; to perform jobs requiring precise attainment of set limits, tolerances or standards.

VII. ABILITY TO MAKE GENERALIZATIONS, EVALUATIONS OR DECISIONS WITHOUT IMMEDIATE SUPERVISION .... ☐ ☒

The ability to retain awareness of potential hazards and observe appropriate precautions; to understand and remember detailed instructions; to travel in unfamiliar places or use public transportation systems.

VIII. ABILITY TO ACCEPT AND CARRY OUT RESPONSIBILITY FOR DIRECTION, CONTROL AND PLANNING .... ☐ ☒

The ability to set realistic goals or make plans independently of others; to negotiate with, instruct or supervise people; to respond appropriately to changes in the work setting.

APPENDIX C

SAMPLE JOB DESCRIPTIONS

- CONSTRUCTION TRADES
- TRUCK DRIVER, SEMI
- CUSTODIAN I

JOB DESCRIPTION

Position Title: _PAINTER_

Job Code/Labor Grade: _872/MT-I_

Department/Division: _PAINTING_

Work Unit: _SPECIALTY CREW_   NO. of EE's: _1_

Shift Assignment: A _____   B _X_____   C _____

Union Affiliation: _NONE_

Supervisor: _BRUCE STONE_   Phone Number: _213-7300 EXT. 024_

Job Analyst: _R. THRUSH_   Phone Number: _000-0000_

ESSENTIAL FUNCTIONS STATEMENT

Purpose: _TO APPLY PAINT TO STREETS, PARKING, PLAYGROUND, INSTRUCTIONAL AREAS AND STRUCTURES._

Functions: _1. DETERMINES PAINTING OPERATIONS TO COMPLY WITH WRITTEN AND VERBAL INSTRUCTIONS AND TRADE PRACTICES._

2. PREPARES PAINTING SURFACES TO ENSURE ADHESION OF PRIMER AND FINISH COATS OF PAINT USING SCRAPERS, ELECTRIC SANDERS AND CLEANING SOLUTIONS.

3. APPLIES PAINT TO METAL, WOOD, BRICK, CONCRETE, DRYWALL AND ASPHALT SURFACES USING HAND ROLLER, BRUSH, AIRLESS SPRAYPAINT APPARATUS AND STRIPPING MACHINE.

4. SETS UP LADDERS & SCAFFOLDING TO ENSURE SAFE ABOVE GROUND WORK PLATFORM.

(MORE ON NEXT PAGE)

Write additional functions on the Essential Functions Supplementary List.

JOB QUALIFICATIONS

Education: _HIGH SCHOOL GRADUATE_

Experience: _2 YEARS EXPERIENCE UNDER JOURNEYMAN PAINTER_

Skills/Knowledge/Abilities: _KNOWLEDGE OF METHODS, TOOLS, EQUIPMENT, MATERIALS AND MEANS OF PAINTING. ABILITY TO READ BLUEPRINTS AND ESTIMATE MATERIALS REQUIRED FOR ORDERS_

Licenses/Certificates: _VALID DRIVERS LICENSE._

Machine, Equipment, Tool Skills: _AIRLESS SPRAYER, ORBITAL SANDER, HANDTOOLS, LADDERS, SCRAPERS, PAINT BRUSHES AND ROLLERS, AND MASKING MATERIALS._

JOB DESCRIPTION—ESSENTIAL FUNCTIONS CONTINUED

List additional functions, (continued from page 1 of form).

5. DRIVES CREW VEHICLE TO TRANSPORT CREW, EQUIPMENT AND SUPPLIES TO THE JOB SITE.

JOB REQUIREMENTS

PHYSICAL REQUIREMENTS

	NUMBER OF HOURS				
	0	0-3	3-5	5-8	8+
1. SITTING	☐	☒	☐	☐	☐
2. STANDING	☐	☒	☐	☐	☐
3. WALKING	☐	☐	☒	☐	☐
4. REACHING OVERHEAD	☐	☒	☐	☐	☐
5. BENDING OVER	☐	☐	☐	☒	☐
6. CROUCHING	☐	☐	☐	☒	☐
7. KNEELING	☐	☐	☒	☐	☐
8. CRAWLING	☐	☒	☐	☐	☐
9. CLIMBING	☐	☒	☐	☐	☐
10. BALANCING	☐	☒	☐	☐	☐
11. PUSHING/PULLING	☐	☐	☐	☒	☐
12. LIFTING/CARRYING					
A. 10 LBS OR LESS	☐	☐	☐	☒	☐
B. 11-25 LBS	☐	☐	☒	☐	☐
C. 25-50 LBS	☐	☒	☐	☐	☐
D. 51-75 LBS	☐	☒	☐	☐	☐
E. 76-100 LBS	☒	☐	☐	☐	☐
F. OVER 100 LBS	☒	☐	☐	☐	☐
13. DRIVING	☐	☒	☐	☐	☐
14. REPETITIVE USE-FOOT					
A. RIGHT ONLY	☐	☒	☐	☐	☐
B. LEFT ONLY	☒	☐	☐	☐	☐
C. BOTH	☐	☐	☐	☐	☐

	NUMBER OF HOURS				
	0	0-3	3-5	5-8	8+
15. REPETITIVE USE–HAND					
A. DOMINANT	☐	☐	☐	☐	☐
B. NON-DOMINANT	☐	☐	☐	☐	☐
C. BOTH	☐	☐	☐	☒	☐
16. GRASPING-LIGHT					
A. DOMINANT	☒	☐	☐	☐	☐
B. NON-DOMINANT	☒	☐	☐	☐	☐
C. BOTH	☐	☐	☐	☐	☐
GRASPING-FIRM/STRONG					
D. DOMINANT	☐	☐	☐	☐	☐
E. NON-DOMINANT	☐	☐	☐	☐	☐
F. BOTH	☐	☐	☐	☒	☐
17. FINGER DEXTERITY					
A. DOMINANT	☐	☒	☐	☐	☐
B. NON-DOMINANT	☒	☐	☐	☐	☐
C. BOTH	☐	☐	☐	☐	☐
18. VISION					
A. ACUITY, FAR	☐	☐	☐	☒	☐
B. ACUITY, NEAR	☐	☐	☐	☒	☐
C. DEPTH PERCEPTION	☒	☐	☐	☐	☐
D. FIELD OF VISION	☒	☐	☐	☐	☐
E. ACCOMMODATION	☒	☐	☐	☐	☐
F. COLOR VISION	☐	☒	☐	☐	☐

Mental Requirements

☐ Reading, Simple	☒ Spatial	☒ Tending
☒ Reading, Complex	☒ Form	☒ Precision Working
☒ Writing, Simple	☐ Clerical	☒ Follow Instructions
☐ Writing, Complex	☐ Compiling	☒ Influence Others
☐ Math Skills, Simple	☒ Coordination	☒ Time Requirement
☒ Math Skills, Complex	☒ Analyzing	☒ Memorization
☒ Tasks, Simple	☐ Synthesizing	☒ Problem Solving
☒ Tasks, Complex	☐ Supervising	☒ Independent Judgement
	☐ Instructing	☒ Decision Making
	☒ Driving	

Work Environment

☒ Works Alone	☒ Confined Areas	☒ Electrical Devices
☒ Works with Others	☐ Extreme Heat	☒ Mechanical Devices
☒ Works Around Others	☐ Extreme Cold	☐ Computer Equipment
☒ Verbal Contact w/Others	☐ Wet and/or Humid	☐ Pneumatic Devices
☒ Face-to-Face Contact	☒ Noise	☐ Flame/Heat Generated
☐ Shift Work	☐ Vibration	Devices
☐ Extended Day	☒ Solvents/Oils	☐ Moving Objects
☒ Inside	☒ Fumes/Odors	☒ High Places
☒ Outside	☒ Dirt/Dust	☒ Slippery Surfaces
	☒ Gases	
	☐ Explosives	

Analyst Name ___R. THRUSH___ Date ___NOV. 10, 1992___

Supervisors Name ___B. STONE___ Date ___NOV. 12, 1992___

Approval Date ___NOV. 20, 1992___

JOB DESCRIPTION

Position Title: _TRUCK DRIVER_

Job Code/Labor Grade: _985/MB_

Department/Division: _SHIPPING_

Work Unit: _TRANSPORTATION_ NO. of EE's: _6_

Shift Assignment: A _____ B _X_ C _____

Union Affiliation: _INTERNATIONAL SOCIETY OF TRUCK DRIVERS_

Supervisor: _CHUCK FLEMMING_ Phone Number: _000-0000_

Job Analyst: _R. THRUSH_ Phone Number: _000-0000_

ESSENTIAL FUNCTIONS STATEMENT

Purpose: _TO TRANSPORT CARGO,._

Functions: _1. DRIVES SEMI-TRACTOR TRAILERS TO TRANSPORT OVERSIZED CARGO._
2. DRIVES TRUCKS TO PICK UP AND DELIVER CARGO AT DESIGNATED LOCATIONS.
3. VERIFIES AND SECURES CARGO TO ENSURE SAFE TRANSPORT.

Write additional functions on the Essential Functions Supplementary List.

JOB QUALIFICATIONS

Education: _HIGH SCHOOL GRADUATE_

Experience: _MINIMUM 5 YEARS EXPERIENCE DRIVING TRACTOR-TRAILERS AND TRUCKS._

Skills/Knowledge/Abilities: _KNOWLEDGE OF DEPARTMENT OF TRANSPORTATION CARGO TRANSPORT RULES, REGULATIONS AND POLICIES._

Licenses/Certificates: _TRUCK DRIVERS LICENSE WITH CURRENT HEALTH CARD._

Machine, Equipment, Tool Skills: _18 SPEED DIESEL TRACTOR, CONTAINER, FLATBED AND TANDEM TRAILERS, PICKUP TRUCKS, BOBTAIL TRUCKS, FORKLIFT, TWO-WAY RADIO, HAND TRUCK, CARGO TIE DOWNS._

JOB REQUIREMENTS

PHYSICAL REQUIREMENTS

NUMBER OF HOURS	0	0-3	3-5	5-8	8+
1. SITTING	☐	☐	☒	☐	☐
2. STANDING	☐	☒	☐	☐	☐
3. WALKING	☐	☒	☐	☐	☐
4. REACHING OVERHEAD	☐	☒	☐	☐	☐
5. BENDING OVER	☐	☒	☐	☐	☐
6. CROUCHING	☐	☒	☐	☐	☐
7. KNEELING	☐	☒	☐	☐	☐
8. CRAWLING	☒	☐	☐	☐	☐
9. CLIMBING	☐	☒	☐	☐	☐
10. BALANCING	☐	☒	☐	☐	☐
11. PUSHING/PULLING	☐	☐	☒	☐	☐
12. LIFTING/CARRYING					
A. 10 LBS OR LESS	☐	☐	☒	☐	☐
B. 11-25 LBS	☐	☐	☒	☐	☐
C. 25-50 LBS	☐	☒	☐	☐	☐
D. 51-75 LBS	☒	☐	☐	☐	☐
E. 76-100 LBS	☒	☐	☐	☐	☐
F. OVER 100 LBS	☒	☐	☐	☐	☐
13. DRIVING	☐	☐	☒	☐	☐
14. REPETITIVE USE-FOOT					
A. RIGHT ONLY	☐	☐	☐	☐	☐
B. LEFT ONLY	☐	☐	☐	☐	☐
C. BOTH	☐	☐	☒	☐	☐

NUMBER OF HOURS	0	0-3	3-5	5-8	8+
15. REPETITIVE USE–HAND					
A. DOMINANT	☐	☐	☐	☒	☐
B. NON-DOMINANT	☐	☐	☒	☐	☐
C. BOTH	☐	☐	☐	☐	☐
16. GRASPING-LIGHT					
A. DOMINANT	☐	☐	☐	☐	☐
B. NON-DOMINANT	☐	☐	☐	☐	☐
C. BOTH	☒	☐	☐	☐	☐
GRASPING-FIRM/STRONG					
D. DOMINANT	☐	☐	☐	☒	☐
E. NON-DOMINANT	☐	☐	☒	☐	☐
F. BOTH	☐	☐	☐	☐	☐
17. FINGER DEXTERITY					
A. DOMINANT	☐	☐	☐	☐	☐
B. NON-DOMINANT	☐	☐	☐	☐	☐
C. BOTH	☐	☒	☐	☐	☐
18. VISION					
A. ACUITY, FAR	☐	☐	☒	☐	☐
B. ACUITY, NEAR	☐	☐	☒	☐	☐
C. DEPTH PERCEPTION	☐	☐	☒	☐	☐
D. FIELD OF VISION	☐	☐	☒	☐	☐
E. ACCOMMODATION	☐	☐	☒	☐	☐
F. COLOR VISION	☒	☐	☐	☐	☐

MENTAL REQUIREMENTS

☒	Reading, Simple	☒	Spatial	❑	Tending
❑	Reading, Complex	❑	Form	❑	Precision Working
☒	Writing, Simple	❑	Clerical	☒	Follow Instructions
❑	Writing, Complex	❑	Compiling	❑	Influence Others
❑	Math Skills, Simple	❑	Coordination	☒	Time Requirement
☒	Math Skills, Complex	❑	Analyzing	☒	Memorization
☒	Tasks, Simple	❑	Synthesizing	❑	Problem Solving
❑	Tasks, Complex	❑	Supervising	☒	Independent Judgement
		❑	Instructing	❑	Decision Making
		☒	Driving		

WORK ENVIRONMENT

☒	Works Alone	❑	Confined Areas	❑	Electrical Devices
☒	Works with Others	❑	Extreme Heat	☒	Mechanical Devices
☒	Works Around Others	❑	Extreme Cold	❑	Computer Equipment
☒	Verbal Contact w/Others	❑	Wet and/or Humid	❑	Pneumatic Devices
☒	Face-to-Face Contact	☒	Noise	❑	Flame/Heat Generated
❑	Shift Work	☒	Vibration		Devices
☒	Extended Day	❑	Solvents/Oils	☒	Moving Objects
☒	Inside	❑	Fumes/Odors	☒	High Places
☒	Outside	❑	Dirt/Dust	☒	Slippery Surfaces
		❑	Gases		
		❑	Explosives		

Analyst Name ___R. THRUSH___ Date ___7-1-92___

Supervisors Name ___C. FLEMMING___ Date ___7-2-92___

Approval Date ___7-1-92___

JOB DESCRIPTION

Position Title: _CUSTODIAN I_

Job Code/Labor Grade: _664/2_

Department/Division: _OPERATIONS_

Work Unit: _CUSTODIAL_ NO. of EE's: _12_

Shift Assignment: A _____ B _____ C _X_

Union Affiliation: _NONE_

Supervisor: _MIKE PITTS_ Phone Number: _000-0000_

Job Analyst: _R. THRUSH_ Phone Number: _000-0000_

ESSENTIAL FUNCTIONS STATEMENT

Purpose: _TO ENSURE ASSIGNED AREAS ARE CLEAN, SECURE, ORDERLY AND SAFE._

Functions: _1. CLEANS FLOORS, WALLS, CARPETS, FURNITURE, AND WALKWAYS TO REMOVE DIRT, DEBRIS AND SPILLS USING RAGS, BROOMS, MOPS, VACUUM, BUFFER AND CLEANING SOLUTIONS._

2. DISINFECTS BATHROOMS, SHOWERS, AND PUBLIC AREAS TO REMOVE AND INHIBIT THE GROWTH OF BACTERIA AND GERMS USING RAGS, BRUSHES, BROOMS, MOPS, GLOVES, AND CLEANING SOLUTIONS.

3. INSPECTS DOORS, WINDOWS, LOCKS, LIGHTS AND EQUIPMENT TO SAFEGUARD PROPERTY USING KEYS, LOCKS AND FLASHLIGHT. (MORE ON NEXT PAGE).

Write additional functions on the Essential Functions Supplementary List.

JOB QUALIFICATIONS

Education: _HIGH SCHOOL GRADUATE_

Experience: _SIX MONTHS GENERAL CLEANING EXPERIENCE._

Skills/Knowledge/Abilities: _KNOWLEDGE OF STANDARD CLEANING PROCEDURES AND STANDARD CLEANING AGENTS. ABILITY TO DEMONSTRATE KNOWLEDGE AND EXPERIENCE OF CUSTODIAL ACTIVITIES._

Licenses/Certificates: _VALID DRIVERS LICENSE_

Machine, Equipment, Tool Skills: _RAGS, BROOMS, BRUSHES, MOPS, VACUUM CLEANER, GLOVES, BUFFER, CLEANING SOLUTIONS, KEYS, FLASHLIGHT._

JOB DESCRIPTION—ESSENTIAL FUNCTIONS CONTINUED

List additional functions, (continued from page 1 of form).

4. ARRANGES FURNITURE AND EQUIPMENT TO ORGANIZE ROOMS FOR EVENTS AND MEETINGS USING CARTS, DOLLIES AND ELECTRIC CART.

5. REPLENISHES PAPER, LIQUID AND POWDER DISPENSERS TO ENSSURE ADEQUATE SUPPLY ON HAND USING SMALL HAND TOOLS, KEYS AND FUNNEL.

6. REPORTS SANITARY AND SAFETY HAZARDS, VANDALISM, AND UNAUTHORIZED PERSONNEL TO ENHANCE THE HEALTH AND SAFETY OF STUDENTS, STAFF AND THE PUBLIC USING TELEPHONE, SIGNS, FORMS, TAGS AND WRITING UTENSILS.

JOB REQUIREMENTS

PHYSICAL REQUIREMENTS

Number of Hours	0	0-3	3-5	5-8	8+
1. SITTING	☐	☒	☐	☐	☐
2. STANDING	☐	☒	☐	☐	☐
3. WALKING	☐	☐	☐	☒	☐
4. REACHING OVERHEAD	☐	☒	☐	☐	☐
5. BENDING OVER	☐	☒	☐	☐	☐
6. CROUCHING	☐	☒	☐	☐	☐
7. KNEELING	☐	☒	☐	☐	☐
8. CRAWLING	☒	☐	☐	☐	☐
9. CLIMBING	☐	☒	☐	☐	☐
10. BALANCING	☐	☒	☐	☐	☐
11. PUSHING/PULLING	☐	☐	☐	☒	☐
12. LIFTING/CARRYING					
A. 10 LBS OR LESS	☐	☐	☐	☒	☐
B. 11-25 LBS	☐	☐	☒	☐	☐
C. 25-50 LBS	☐	☒	☐	☐	☐
D. 51-75 LBS	☒	☐	☐	☐	☐
E. 76-100 LBS	☒	☐	☐	☐	☐
F. OVER 100 LBS	☒	☐	☐	☐	☐
13. DRIVING	☒	☐	☐	☐	☐
14. REPETITIVE USE-FOOT					
A. RIGHT ONLY	☒	☐	☐	☐	☐
B. LEFT ONLY	☒	☐	☐	☐	☐
C. BOTH	☒	☐	☐	☐	☐

Number of Hours	0	0-3	3-5	5-8	8+
15. REPETITIVE USE–HAND					
A. DOMINANT	☐	☐	☐	☒	☐
B. NON-DOMINANT	☐	☐	☒	☐	☐
C. BOTH	☐	☐	☐	☐	☐
16. GRASPING-LIGHT					
A. DOMINANT	☒	☐	☐	☐	☐
B. NON-DOMINANT	☒	☐	☐	☐	☐
C. BOTH	☐	☐	☐	☐	☐
GRASPING-FIRM/STRONG					
D. DOMINANT	☐	☐	☐	☒	☐
E. NON-DOMINANT	☐	☐	☒	☐	☐
F. BOTH	☐	☐	☐	☐	☐
17. FINGER DEXTERITY					
A. DOMINANT	☐	☐	☐	☐	☐
B. NON-DOMINANT	☐	☐	☐	☐	☐
C. BOTH	☐	☒	☐	☐	☐
18. VISION					
A. ACUITY, FAR	☐	☐	☐	☒	☐
B. ACUITY, NEAR	☐	☐	☐	☒	☐
C. DEPTH PERCEPTION	☒	☐	☐	☐	☐
D. FIELD OF VISION	☒	☐	☐	☐	☐
E. ACCOMMODATION	☒	☐	☐	☐	☐
F. COLOR VISION	☒	☐	☐	☐	☐

MENTAL REQUIREMENTS

☒ Reading, Simple	☐ Spatial	☐ Tending
☐ Reading, Complex	☐ Form	☐ Precision Working
☒ Writing, Simple	☐ Clerical	☒ Follow Instructions
☐ Writing, Complex	☐ Compiling	☐ Influence Others
☒ Math Skills, Simple	☐ Coordination	☒ Time Requirement
☐ Math Skills, Complex	☐ Analyzing	☐ Memorization
☒ Tasks, Simple	☐ Synthesizing	☐ Problem Solving
☐ Tasks, Complex	☐ Supervising	☐ Independent Judgement
	☐ Instructing	☐ Decision Making
	☐ Driving	

WORK ENVIRONMENT

☒ Works Alone	☐ Confined Areas	☒ Electrical Devices
☒ Works with Others	☐ Extreme Heat	☐ Mechanical Devices
☐ Works Around Others	☐ Extreme Cold	☐ Computer Equipment
☐ Verbal Contact w/Others	☐ Wet and/or Humid	☐ Pneumatic Devices
☒ Face-to-Face Contact	☐ Noise	☐ Flame/Heat Generated
☐ Shift Work	☐ Vibration	Devices
☐ Extended Day	☐ Solvents/Oils	☐ Moving Objects
☒ Inside	☒ Fumes/Odors	☐ High Places
☐ Outside	☒ Dirt/Dust	☒ Slippery Surfaces
	☒ Gases	
	☐ Explosives	

Analyst Name   _R. THRUSH_   Date _2-3-93_

Supervisors Name _M. PITTS_   Date _2-3-93_

Approval Date   _2-10-93_

APPENDIX D

WORKER TRAIT DEFINITIONS

Terms used on the *"Essential Functions—Demands Job Analysis Worksheet"* are defined to enhance their uniform interpretation and consistent completion of the worksheet.

WORKER - TRAIT DEFINITIONS

The following terms and definitions are from the U.S. Department of Labor publication, *"Revised Handbook for Analyzing Jobs,"* 1992 edition. These terms are commonly used for describing requirements and qualifications required in industry. Notations in paraenthesis are direct references to the Essential Funtions—Demands Job Analysis worksheet.

JOB REQUIREMENTS—PHYSICAL FACTORS

Factor 1—Mobility

Standing: Remaining on one's feet in an upright position at a work station without moving about.

Walking: Moving about on foot.

Sitting: Remaining in a seated position.

Factor 1—Lifting, Carrying, Pushing, Pulling

Lifting: Raising or lowering an object vertically from one level to another (includes upward pulling).

Carrying: Transporting an object horizontally, usually holding it in the hands or arms or on the shoulder.

Pushing: Exerting force upon an object so that the object moves away from the force (includes slapping, striking, kicking, and treadle actions).

Pulling: Exerting force upon an object so that the object moves toward the force (includes jerking).

Factor 2—Agility

Climbing: Ascending or descending ladders, stairs, scaffolding, ramps, poles, and the like, using feet and legs or hands and arms. Body agility is emphasized. Be descriptive in terms of height, number of steps, steepness, duration, and type of structure climbed.

Balancing: Maintaining body equilibrium to prevent falling when walking, standing, crouching, or running on narrow, slippery, or erratically moving surfaces; or maintaining body equilibrium when performing gymnastic feats. Be descriptive in terms of type or condition of surface and activities during which balance must be maintained.

Stooping: Bending body downward and forward by forward flexing the spine at the waist and the lower extremities, requiring full use of the lower extremities and back muscles. Be descriptive in terms of duration.

Bending: Flexing the lower back forward and downward with minimal flexion of the lower extremities. Be descriptive in terms of duration.

Kneeling: Bending legs at knees to come to rest one knee or both knees. Be descriptive in terms of duration.

Crouching: Bending body downward and forward by forward flexing legs and spine. Be descriptive in terms of duration.

Crawling: Moving about on hands and knees or hands and feet. Be descriptive in terms of distance and duration.

Twisting: Rotation of the lower trunk without movement of lower extremities. Be descriptive in terms of duration.

Turning: Rotation on the ball of one foot or both feet to reposition whole body. Be descriptive in terms of frequency.

Factor 3—Dexterity

Reaching: Extending hand(s) and arm(s) in any direction. (Reaching forward or reaching overhead).

Handling: Seizing, holding, grasping, turning, or otherwise working with hand or hands. Fingers are involved only to the extent that they are an extension of the hand, such as to shift automobile gears. (Grasping firm/strong or grasping light).

Fingering: Picking, **pinching**, or otherwise working primarily with fingers rather than with the whole hand or arm.

Factor 4—Coordination

Coordination: Coordinated use of controls entail use of one or both arms or hands **(hand-arm)** or one or both feet or legs **(foot-leg)** to move controls on machinery or equipment. In this sub-item, the analyst must consider whether the worker moves controls on the machine or equipment by using either right side body members, left side body members, or members of either or both sides. In addition, the use of hand-arm controls is distinguished from use of foot-leg controls. Controls include, but are not limited to, buttons, knobs, pedals, levers, and cranks. (Eye–hand or eye–hand–foot).

Driving: Operating vehicles requiring use of vision and foot and hand controls.

Factor 5—Vision

Near Acuity: Clarity of vision at 20 inches or less.

Far Acuity: Clarity of vision at 20 feet or more.

Depth Perception: Three-dimensional vision. Ability to judge distances and spatial relationships so as to see objects where and as they actually are.

Accommodation: Adjustment of lens of eye to bring an object into sharp focus. This factor is required when doing near point work at varying distances from the eye.

Color Vision: Ability to identify and distinguish colors.

Field of Vision: Observing an area that can be seen up and down or to right or left while eyes are fixed on given point.

Factor 6—Talking

Talking: Expressing or exchanging ideas by means of the spoken word to impart oral information to clients or to the **public** and to convey detailed spoken instructions to other workers accurately, loudly, or quickly.

Factor 7—Hearing

Hearing: Perceiving the nature of sounds by ear.

Job Requirements - Environmental Factors

Exposure to Weather:	Exposure to outside atmospheric conditions. (A and B)
Extreme Cold:	Exposure to nonweather-related cold temperatures. (C)
Extreme Heat:	Exposure to nonweather-related hot temperatures. (C)
Wet and/or Humid:	Contact with water or other liquids or exposures to nonweather-related humid conditions. (F)
Noise Intensity Level:	The noise intensity level to which the worker is exposed in the job environment. This factor is expressed by one of five levels. Consider all the benchmarks within a level as providing an insight into the nature of the specific levels. (I)
Vibrations:	Exposure to a shaking object or surface. (P)
Atmospheric Conditions:	Exposure to conditions such as fumes, noxious odors, dusts, mists, gases, and poor ventilation, that affect the respiratory system, eyes, or the skin. (G)
Proximity to Moving Mechanical Parts:	Exposure to possible bodily injury from moving mechanical parts of equipment, tools, or machinery. (E)
Exposure to Electrical Shock:	Exposure to possible injury from electrical shock. (J)
Working in High, Exposed Places:	Exposure to possible bodily injury from falling. (D)
Exposure to Radiation:	Exposure to possible bodily injury from radiation. (J)
Working with Explosives:	Exposure to possible injury from explosions. (O)
Exposure to Toxic or Caustic Chemicals:	Exposure to possible bodily injury from toxic or caustic chemicals. (H)
Other Environmental Conditions:	Other environmental conditions, not defined above found in environment. (K, L, M, N, R, S, T)

JOB QUALIFICATIONS—MENTAL FACTORS

Factor 5—Perception

Spatial:	Ability to think visually of geometric forms and to comprehend the two-dimensional representation of three-dimensional objects. The ability to recognize the relationships resulting from the movement of objects in space.
Form:	Ability to perceive pertinent detail in objects or in pictorial or graphic material. Ability to make visual comparisons and discriminations and see slight differences in shapes and shadings of figures and widths and lengths of lines.
Clerical:	Ability to perceive pertinent detail in verbal or tabular material. Ability to observe differences in copy, to proofread words and numbers, and to avoid perceptual errors in arithmetic computation. A measure of speed of perception is required in many industrial jobs even when the job does not have verbal or numerical content.

Factor 6—Data

Synthesizing:	Integrating analyses of data to discover facts and/or develop knowledge concepts or interpretations.
Coordinating:	Determining time, place, and sequence of operations or action to be taken on the basis of analysis of data: executing determination and/or reporting on events.
Analyzing:	Examining and evaluating data. Presenting alternative actions in relation to the evaluation is frequently involved.
Compiling:	Gathering, collating, or classifying information about data, people, or things. Reporting and/or carrying out a prescribed action in relation to the information is frequently involved.
Computing:	Performing arithmetic operations and reporting on and/or carrying out a prescribed action in relation to them. Does not include counting.

Copying: Transcribing, entering, or posting data.

Comparing: Judging the readily observable functional, structural, or compositional characteristics (whether similar to or divergent from obvious standards) or data, people, or things.

Factor 7—People

Mentoring: Dealing with individuals in terms of their total personality in order to advise, counsel, and/or guide them with regard to problems that may be resolved by legal, scientific, clinical, spiritual and/or other professional principles.

Negotiating: Exchanging ideas, information, and opinions with others to formulate policies and programs and/or arrive jointly at decisions, conclusions or solutions.

Instruction: Teaching subject matter to others, or training others (including animals) through explanation, demonstration, and supervised practice; or making recommendations on the basis of technical discipline.

Supervising: Determining or interpreting work procedures for a group of workers, assigning specific duties to them, maintaining harmonious relations among them, and promoting efficiency. A variety of responsibilities is involved in this function.

Diverting: Amusing others. (usually accomplished through the medium of stage, screen, television, or radio).

Persuading: Influencing others in favor of a product, service, or point of view.

Speaking— Signaling: Talking with and/or signaling people to convey or exchange information. Includes giving assignments and/or directions to helpers or assistants.

Serving: Attending to the needs or requests of people or animals or the expressed or implicit wishes of people. Immediate response is involved.

Talking Instructions— Helping: Helping applies to "non-learning" helpers. No variety of responsibility is involved in this function.

Factor 8—Things

Setting Up: Adjusting machines or equipment by replacing or altering tools, jigs, fixtures, and attachments to prepare them to perform their functions, change their performance, or restore their proper functioning if they break down. Workers who set up and personally operate a variety of machines are included here.

Precision Working: Using body members and/or tools or work aids to work, move, guide, or place objects or materials in situations where ultimate responsibility for the attainment of standards occur and selection of appropriate tools, objects or materials, and the adjustment of the tool to the task require exercise of considerable judgment.

Operating—Controlling: Starting, stopping, controlling, and adjusting the progress of machines or equipment. Operating machines involves setting up and adjusting the machine or material(s) as the work progresses. Controlling involves observing gauges, dials, etc., and turning valves and other devices to regulate factors such as temperature, pressure, flow of liquids, speed of pumps, and reactions of materials.

Driving—Operation: Starting, stopping, controlling the actions of machines or equipment for which a course must be steered, or which must be guided, in order fabricate, process, and/or move things for people. Involves such activities as observing gauges and dials; estimating distance and determining speed and direction of other objects; turning cranks and wheels; pushing or pulling gear lifts or levels. Includes such machines as cranes, conveyor systems, tractors, furnace charging machines, paving machines and hoisting machines. Excludes manually powered machines, such as handtrucks and dollies, and power assisted machines, such as electric wheelbarrows and handtrucks.

Manipulating: Using body members, tools, or special devices to work, move, guide, or place objects or materials. Involves some latitude for judgment with regard to precision attained and selecting appropriate tool, object, or material, although this is readily manifest.

Tending: Starting, stopping, and observing the functioning of machines and equipment. Involves adjusting materials or controls of

the machines, such as changing guides, adjusting timers, and temperature gauges, turning valves to allow flow of materials, and flipping switches in response to lights. Little judgment is involved in making these adjustments.

Feeding—Offbearing: Inserting, throwing, dumping, or placing materials in or removing them from machines or equipment which are automatic or tendered or operated by other workers.

Handling: Using body members, handtools, and/or special devices to work, move, or carry objects of materials. Involves little or no latitude for judgment with regard to attainment of standards or in selecting appropriate tool, object, or material.

FUNCTIONAL VERBS

A partial list of action verbs useful for starting functions (duties/tasks) concisely.

FUNCTIONAL VERBS

The following verbs are useful in stating the functions of positions concisely. This partial list is intended to help you avoid the use of vague or ambiguous expressions.

Adept	Modify or change to fit specific or new situations.
Administer	Manage or direct. (Generally requires some additional explanation to show specific detail. (See manage.)
Advise	Offer an informed opinion or give specialized information to others.
Analyze	Identify the elements of a whole and critically examine and relate these component parts separately and/or in relation to the whole.
Allocate	Assign or apportion for a specific purpose or to a particular person.
Appraise	Judge as to quality; compare critically with established standards.Approve Exercise final and decisive authority, causing action to use money, manpower, materials,or equipment.
Assemble	Gather from various sources.
Assign	Specify or designate tasks and duties to be performed by others.
Authorize	Approve or commit an act implying subsequent action by others.
Commit	Pledge or assign to a particular course of action.
Compile	Put together information or assemble data in a new form.
Conduct	Manage or carry on, with emphasis on concept of immediate supervision or personal leadership.
Control	Direct, regulate, or guide the use of money, methods, equipment, materials. Also, the process of monitoring activities to ensure conformance with planned results.
Cooperate	Act jointly with others.
Coordinate	Regulate, adjust or direct the related actions of others in order to attain desired results.

Create	Produce through imaginative skill.
Delegate	Entrust to another person tasks or duties which require exercise of some of the authority of the person originally responsible, as "to delegate an administrative assistant to represent the department at conferences."
Develop	Disclose, discover, perfect, or unfold a plan or idea, in detail, gradually. Implies study and/or experiment unless otherwise stated. When used as "to develop subordinates," see train.
Devise	Form in the mind by combinations of ideas, new applications of principles, or new arrangements of parts.
Direct	Govern or control work operations by establishing and implementing objectives, practices, and methods.
Estimate	Forecast future quantities, values, sizes, extents, etc., either on the basis of judgment or calculations. Frequently, estimating is shared with others, in which case it is more precise touse "estimate" as a noun, and to state the job'sfunction in relation thereto, i.e., originates, analyzes, endorses, approves, etc., estimates of...
Execute	Put into effect or carry out methods, plans, etc.
Forecast	Predict future events based on specified assumptions.
Implement	Carry out or fulfill by taking action.
Improve	Make better.
Inform	Communicate knowledge to others.
Initiate	Set going or introduce.
Inspect	Examine materials, equipment, reports, work, etc., to determine quality, suitability for use, etc.
Instruct	Teach, demonstrate, or by other methods impart knowledge to others. Direct that a specific activity be performed; may include directing how it is to be performed.
Interpret	Explain to others (orally or in writing) the meaning or significance of something.

Investigate	Uncover facts by systematically finding them, conducting a searching inquiry, and examining various sources.
Maintain	Keep in satisfactory condition.
Manage	Plan, organize, direct, control, and evaluate operation of an organizational unit, with responsibility for the output.
Negotiate	Confer with others to reach an agreement.
Originate	Begin or initiate.
Oversee	Supervise a function or operation as distinct from supervising people.
Propose	Recommend or suggest for consideration or adoption.
Recommend	Present a matter to another person for action or approval.
Research	Specific inquiry involving prolonged and critical investigation, having for its aim the study of new facts and their interpretation, the revision of accepted conclusions or theories that may be affected by newly discovered facts,or the practical application of such new or revised conclusions. Example: Technical research to develop new products for the company.
Review	Consider or examine facts or results for accuracy, completeness, and suitability.
Select	Choose that which appears to be best suited for a specific purpose.
Specify	State precisely, or in detail, or name explicitly. Frequently, the function of specifying is shared with others, in which case it is more precise to use the noun "specification" and state of job's functions in relation thereto, i.e., originates, analyzes, endorses, approves, etc. Specifications for...
Supervise	Personally oversee or control work performance and conduct of others, where there is opportunity for control or inspection of work performed.

APPENDIX F

BIBLIOGRAPHY

BIBLIOGRAPHY

Cascio, W., Human Resource Planning, Employment & Placement. Washington, D.C.: Bureau of National Affairs, 1989.

Chaffin, D., Preventing Overexertion Injuries to the Back and Handin Industry. Irvine: University of California, Irvine, 1983.

Drillis, R., and R. Contini, "Body Segment Parameters." Technical Report No. 1166.03. New York: New York University, September, 1966.

CAIRE. Ergonomic Analysis of the Workplace. Eugene, Oregon: 1991.

Federal News Service. "Press Conference with Equal Employment Opportunity Commission," July 25, 1991, Federal News Service.

Roebuck, J.J.; K.H.E. Kroemer; W.G. Thompson, Engineering Anthropometric Methods, New York: John Wiley & Sons, 1975.

Thrush, R., Job Analysis for an Industrial Setting. RMA, Irvine, CA: January 1992.

Thrush, R., "Americans with Disability Act (ADA) Essential Function Identification." Ultra-Sounds CPPSIG, American Physical Therapy Association, Vol. 4, pg 2, July/August 1992.

The Applied Job Analysis System in Public Sector Employment, Applied Job Analysis, Inc., Austin, Texas, 1977.

United States Civil Service Commission. Bureau of Inter-Governmental Personnel Programs. Job Analysis, A Guide for State and Local Governments. Washington, D.C.: Government Printing Office, 1992

U. S. Department of Education, National Institute of Handicapped Research, Material Development Center. Physical Demands Job Analysis: A New Approach. Menomonie, Wisconsin: 1981.

U.S. Department of Labor, Manpower Administration. Revised Handbook for Analyzing Jobs, Washington D.C.: Government Printing Office, 1992.

U.S. Department of Labor, Manpower Administration. Dictionary of Occupational Titles. Washington, D.C.: Government Printing Office, 1991.

U.S. Equal Employment Opportunity Commission. "Equal Employment Opportunity for Individuals with Disabilities." Federal Register Vol. 56, July 26, 1991. Washington, D.C.: Government Printing Office, 1991.

U.S. Equal Employment Opportunity Commission. A Technical Assistance Manual on the Employment Provisions (Title) of the Americans with Disabilities Act, Washington, D.C.: Government Printing Office, January 1992.

U. S. House of Representatives, 101th Congress. Americans with Disabilities Act of 1990. Report 101-485, Part 2, Washington, D.C.: Government Printing Office, 1990.

INDEX

ORDER FORM

"Let us tell you how to order this valuable Educational publication."

ADA Essential Function Identification–A Definitive Application of Title–I

Additional copies of this "How To" textbook can be yours today for $37.95 (U.S. funds) each plus shipping & handling and sales tax where applicable. Simply fill out the order form below and send it with a check or money order payable to:

AccessAbility Press
330 South Magnolia, Suite 302
El Cajon, CA 92020-5221

(Please allow 10 days for processing)

The publication(s) will be sent regular mail–book rate. If quicker delivery is preferred, please call us at 619-442-2677 or fax us at 619-442-0428 for delivery rates. Also, **contact us** for special pricing on volume orders (10 or more), and to order blank forms/worksheets for your use.

Ship to : Name _____

Company: _____

Address: _____

City: _____ State: _____ Zip: _____

Telephone: Office _____ Home _____

Please send _____ copies for $37.95 each for a total of $_____

add your local sales tax (for CA residents only) $_____

Shipping and handling ($2.50 for each book mailed) $_____

Total $_____

Method of Payment: ❑ Check ❑ Money Order

Payable to : AccessAbility Press, 330 South Magnolia, Suite 302
El Cajon, CA 92020-5221

Thank You for your interest in our "How To" ADA Title–I Publication!

Woody and Holmes, Inc., provide ADA/Disability Management Consulting and Training.

Please send me more information regarding these services. ❑ Yes ❑ No